Start Again
from
Scratch

A No-Fail Recipe for Reviving Your Marriage

Laine Lawson Craft
with Steve Craft

A Livin' Lively with Laine Production

Editor: Natalie Gillespie
Cover design by Christian and Elise Stella
Cover photograph of authors by Greg Campbell
Page layout and design by Cyndi Clark

ISBN: 978-0-692-41382-1

Printed in the United States of America

A Livin' Lively with Laine Production
4012 Commons Drive, Suite 224 • Destin, Florida 32541

Dedication

Laine:
To my husband Steve and our children,
Steve Jr., Lawson, and Kaylee.
You make my life sweet. All my love forever.

Steve:
To my wife Laine, joined to me by God,
a child of God who had the courage to say,
"Yes, God, I will do that." To God be the glory.

Table of Contents

Foreword

*I*n the early years of our marriage, I often lay in our bed alone, listening for the sound of tires on the driveway, wondering some nights if my husband would come home at all. For a season in our marriage, Phil would go out night after night. He liked to party, and I was left brokenhearted at home. It was taking a big toll on our marriage.

On those nights and during the days in between, I prayed that God would touch Phil's heart. I endured many dark nights alone with the kids, hoping our marriage could be saved. But I never gave up.

I knew God was up in Heaven and He loved us, but I needed Him to help bring Phil back home down here. I wanted God's will to be lived out in our lives. I shed many a tear, and I fought long and hard for our marriage.

That's why Phil and I are thrilled you have picked up Laine and Steve Craft's wonderful book, *Start Again from Scratch: A No-Fail Recipe for Reviving Your Marriage*. Inside these pages, Laine and Steve outline the fresh ingredients and practical directions you need to create a wonderful recipe for the rest of your life. Even if you think your marriage is dead, we are here to tell you it does not have to be. When it seemed like all hope was gone, God moved in a mighty way in our marriage and in Laine and Steve's marriage too.

Just like Laine and Steve, Phil and I had a miraculous touch from God in our lives that you can experience in your lives too. We know God will move in your marriage if you simply take the steps the Crafts have so wisely outlined in this book.

When Phil gave His life to Christ and started a personal walk with God, all my prayers and hard work for our marriage paid off. Instantly, God moved in our lives and in our marriage. God repaired and restored all of those years that were so painful and lonely and lost.

Now Phil and I get to be a living testimony of how good God is to those who follow His will. We are creating an impact not only through the *Duck Dynasty* television series that shows our real family life and love for God, but also a legacy of love for our family that will last for generations to come. We want our children, grandchildren, great-grandchildren and beyond to know that successful marriages that last a lifetime can be realized, no matter how difficult times may get. Our son Alan and his wife Lisa also experienced hope and healing in their lives and marriage, and you'll hear from them on the next page of this Foreword.

They believe, and we do too, that God can restore and revive any marriage if we ask Him to come into our hearts and give him the control of our lives. In this book, Laine and Steve take you up close and personal into the very best and worst times in their marriage. They lay it on the line and tell you step-by-step what it took to completely revive their marriage. Together, they discovered when all hope is gone, that's right where God loves to come in and show what He can do. So dive in and watch your marriage receive a total turnaround!

Blessings on your marriage journey,
Miss Kay and Phil Robertson, *Duck Dynasty*

*Y*es, we know exactly what it's like to watch your marriage fall apart. Like Alan's mom and dad, we had seasons in our marriage that were beyond miserable. Seasons of heartache, infidelity, and pain from the past. In our new book, *A New Season*, we decided to lay our souls bare and let the world know we are not perfect people, just forgiven. And that God is the only one who could have revived our marriage.

That's why we love Laine and Steve Craft's new book *Start Again from Scratch*. The pages you are about to read are packed with so much wise information, so many good ideas and practical tips and techniques. They give you the "Secret Sauce" and so much more to help you turn your marriage around.

If you have picked up this book, you may also be in a true time of despair and hopelessness in your marriage. You may be facing so many challenges and trials that you feel you will never be able to restore your marriage. Hear us when we tell you that is a lie from the enemy of your very souls.

Alan and I found complete restoration in our marriage. We now have a marriage that is better and stronger than we could ever have dreamed or imagined. And as you'll read in this book, Laine and Steve do too. Yes, it took some time for the healing process. Yes, it took some work and a new way of loving in our marriage. But anyone can choose to start again from scratch. Throw out the old, disgusting mess you've made. Just don't throw out the one you made it with. Start over together, and the benefits are beautiful.

I am confident after reading this book, you can have your miracle and live it too! God did it for our marriage and He will do it for yours too. So turn the page and get started. What are you waiting for?

Lisa and Alan Robertson, *Duck Dynasty*

Introduction

Have Your Miracle and Live It Too

When Steve and I got married almost thirty years ago, we never dreamed our first seventeen years would become hell on earth. I never thought there would come a day when I would love to hate my husband. Here was the man I had vowed to love until the day one of us died, and sometimes I wished death would come sooner rather than later.

Maybe you are at that same desperate point in your own marriage. Maybe you think your marriage is so far gone nothing could fix it. Not even a miracle. You don't even know why you picked up this book. But you did pick it up. We're so glad you did.

Inside this book lies the story of the honest-to-goodness miracle that happened in our marriage. We discovered a secret that in a single instant erased years' worth of arguments, mistrust, broken promises, curse words, and hate. In one conversation and one prayer, all the parts of our marriage that we had burned beyond recognition fell away. It happened when Steve and I made a decision together to start again from scratch.

I know that sounds too simple, but believe us, it worked. We got our love back. We kept our family together. We preserved our legacy. We prevented our children's hearts from breaking. We discovered sizzling sex. We became best friends.

The changes stuck too. We started again from scratch twelve years ago, and today our marriage is better than ever. We love each other more, like each other tremendously, and can't wait to live to a ripe old age together.

The best part of our miracle is now we get to share it with you.

Every couple can do the same thing we did and decide together to start again from scratch. That's why we call this the "no-fail recipe for reviving your marriage."

If you grab all the ingredients we suggest and follow the directions carefully (Don't forget a heaping helping of our "Secret Sauce"), in no time at all you'll be cooking up a brand new relationship with your same old spouse. One that tastes better than you ever could have dreamed.

Better than chocolate peanut butter pie. Better than your grandma's sour cream pound cake with buttercream icing. Better than the tastiest filet mignon with homemade burgundy shallot mushroom sauce or the most luscious lobster dripping with butter. We could continue, but the list is making us hungry.

How about it? Are you feeling the hunger pangs for change? Thirsty for a brand new relationship? Tired of living on a marital diet of mistrust, dishonesty, contempt, and criticism? Whether you have been married five months or fifteen years, that kind of negative diet has not made you a lean, mean marriage machine. Nope. Instead, we bet it has packed on the pounds of loneliness, bitterness, and resentment. Every day, you feel heavier and heavier as all the junk in your marital trunk weighs you down.

Today is the day you can shed the extra weight and start again from scratch. Right now. This minute, you and your spouse can experience the same miracle Steve and I had. Sooner than you think, you will be having your miracle and living it too. We can't wait 'til you try a bite.

We are so excited to share with you the ways we learned how to *Start Again from Scratch: A No-Fail Recipe for Reviving Your Marriage*. Inside these chapters, you will find special ingredients that will bring your love back to life. You'll discover directions that will help you combine these fresh ingredients in the very best way to spice up your marriage and make it a sizzling success.

Each chapter of *Start Again from Scratch* contains some of our personal story and a new ingredient or direction for your marriage. The chapters start with my (Laine's) insight, followed by some of Steve's perspective. We thought it was important for couples to hear both sides of the story, from the wife and the husband. As husband and wife, male and female, Steve and I process things differently. We also feel differently and act and react differently. In order to capture the full picture of our marriage restoration, we believe you, the readers, can benefit best from the input of both of us.

At the end of each chapter, you will find a "recipe" of action points for you to take and build upon, plus a "recipe card" journaling page to add your own notes and tweaks. We encourage you to write down what you are doing and feeling as your recipe unfolds. It will be a powerful dish to share with others soon.

Finally, the last page of each chapter is an actual recipe of ours you can carry into your kitchen and try. Food brings comfort, and these are some of our family's favorite no-fail recipes to help fill your stomach and nourish your bodies as you work hard to renew your hearts.

No matter how bad your marriage is today, it can be transformed by tomorrow. We know it can. We're living proof. So please join us now on the journey. We promise if you start again from scratch and follow our no-fail recipe, your marriage will revive and thrive.

Then you can share your miracle story too.

> Livin' Lively with Love,
> *Laine Lawson Craft*

CHAPTER ONE

Burnt to a Crisp

"I was 32 when I started cooking; up until then, I just ate."
Julia Child

Our marriage was over.
Burnt to a crisp.
Toast.
Stick a fork in us and call us done.

Seventeen years after Steve and I joined hands in my mom's backyard and said our "I do's," I now couldn't stand the sight of my husband, the handsome, hardworking scientist I had promised to love 'til death do us part.

And I couldn't live a lie anymore.

With slow footsteps and a heavy heart, I trudged up the

driveway to our garage, dreading what would come next. I was going to confront Steve and tell him point-blank that I was going to have a new life. I was starting over. I was taking the kids and leaving him. Or Steve could agree that we would start again, right that very moment, from scratch.

I thought I knew what his answer would be. I was pretty sure we'd be hiring lawyers and heading to divorce court. Our three young kids would grow up with a broken family, but that had to be better than the bitter words and icy chills they experienced between me and their dad every day.

I'm telling you, our marriage was bad. We yelled. I cried. He cussed. I stormed out. We fought long, and we didn't fight fair. We wounded each other so deeply we didn't even recognize the people we had become. The scars on our hearts were so thick and callused we could have thrown each other out the window and not even cared. After more than fifteen years of dysfunction, we had been poking and jabbing at each other for so long there wasn't a civil bone left in either of our bodies.

I absolutely hated Steve.

And he hated me right back.

Just ask him. He'll tell you.

My wife is right. On a scale of one to ten with ten being the worst, our marriage was at least a nine. Like a good piece of meat that's been left in the fridge for too long, our marriage had spoiled. Frankly, it was bad spoiled and stank to high heaven.

I hated her. Despised, loathed, and any other word you can think of that means I was sick to death of my beautiful blonde bride. My Laine. And when she made me mad, which was on a regular basis. I told her so too. I said, "You are a (insert nasty word here). I hate you. Why don't you just leave?"

After years of a marriage that was anything but wedded bliss, I was sick of the drama. We disagreed about everything. It became a battle. First it was who was gonna wear the pants. Then, who was not working enough, not pulling their weight. "I am working harder than you." If you sat down to rest, well, that would surely precipitate the devil.

I was sick of it all. Sick of the nagging. Sick of the fights. Sick of my own fear our whole family was hanging off the edge of a cliff by our fingernails and I couldn't do anything to save any of us. I couldn't hold on anymore. I was tired. Sick and tired. Sick and tired of being sick and tired. Sick and tired of everything being so hard. And it was all her fault.

When you are standing in the laundry room at the dryer cursing your wife under your breath because you can't find your left sock, convinced it is all her fault, that is resentment. After all those years, I had a lot of resentment. I tell you, I would rather have spent the rest of my life with Satan than spend even one more minute with my wife.

So there I was, headed up the driveway of our Home Not-So-Sweet Home, bone-weary but ready to fight for my life. For my kids' lives.

I didn't love my husband anymore.

I didn't want my husband anymore.

It was high time to throw out the whole burnt-up mess of our marriage and begin a brand new life with fresh ingredients.

I marched up to Steve with head held high and told him we needed to talk. I poured out my heart. I laid it all on the line. Admitted how miserable I felt. Confessed I had been tempted to stray. Told him how lonely I was and how much his harsh words had torn my soul apart.

I told him I was not going to live the lie of a happy marriage anymore, the lie we were doing all right, the lie everything was fine. Not for one more minute. Either I was going to start making all those lies into truths with him right then or I was leaving for good.

I put my husband on the spot. Did he want me to walk out and cook up a new life without him? Or could we find a way to start again from scratch with each other?

The way I looked at it was simple. I was determined to start over, period. No question about that. I was D-O-N-E *done* doing life and marriage the way we had been. But, honestly, didn't it make more sense to start over with the one I started with? I mean, if I was gonna do all the hard work to create a new recipe for my life, wouldn't it be better to do it with the same main ingredient that in the beginning I couldn't get enough of?

I wanted love in my life. I wanted to be cherished and understood. Frankly, after so many years of trying I had no idea if I could ever get that from Steve. But starting over with someone new would be so complicated. I had baggage. Years and years' worth of baggage. Plus, three kids to boot.

A new man might seem exciting at first, but he would never be able to share the memories of our children's births. He would never know the stories of Steve's and my struggles to succeed in business. Some new guy would not understand the battles Steve and I fought to keep our only daughter healthy through years of medical crises.

A new man might look appealing. He might say the sweet words I was dying to hear. But he wouldn't know my likes and dislikes, my quirks and pet peeves. I might hate Steve, but after all those years together at least he knew my habits, my way of doing things.

Not to mention the kids would have to get used to somebody new in their lives. If I married again, they'd have a new man in their home, in their space, in their mom's bedroom. I would have to sacrifice nights, weekends, and holidays without them as they went back and forth between me and their dad.

Plus, Steve and I would still have to deal with each other over parenting decisions. We'd still see each other at school functions, church programs, and special occasions. Eventually, we'd have graduation parties and weddings to plan. I was never going to get away from my husband, even if he became my ex-husband. Not with three children together. I was stuck with him in some ways for life, even if our marriage ended.

"I was never going to *get away* from my husband, even if he became my ex-husband. Not with three children together."

That's why I came to the conclusion if I was going to start my life over from scratch, I would ask Steve to do it with me. It didn't matter that I didn't love him anymore. It didn't matter that he couldn't stand the sight of me.

I knew if we put our minds to it and decided to begin again, somehow we could find some new ingredients to throw in the recipe and make it work. So far in our marriage, like the famous chef Julia Child said, all we'd been doing is eating. We had sat down at the table of our marriage and fought over who got the best parts, the last bite, until there was nothing left of us.

If we started over, we'd have to start cooking together before we could eat. This time, we'd pay a lot more attention to the process. Keep our emotions cooking at the right temperature. If we were both willing, we could pull something out of the oven that was just right this time.

Maybe even delicious.

That night twelve years ago when Laine told me we needed to talk, on the outside I'm sure I looked and sounded pretty angry. On the inside I was shaking. Another fight? Or the final end? Was she packing her things and leaving? Was she taking my kids? And my life? Was she going to yell at the kids to get in the car?

Yes, I hated my wife. How did she think she had the right to take everything away from me in one instant, everything I worked so hard for? Simple, because she wanted to. That power she had, which I was apparently totally unable to fix, made the hate run strong and deep.

I am a scientist. I like the truth. And I never quit. This was not the truth. We had worked too hard. Invested so much. Memories. Hard work. I had no idea how I could swallow one more bite of the disgusting dish of garbage we had cooked up and called a marriage.

But when she began, I knew right away this talk was different. She didn't complain or criticize. This time she was rational, quiet, peaceful, normal. Truthful even, finally! And what she said was new. It was not the same old garbage can. She said she had made a decision to start a new life. And it could be either with somebody else or it could be with me. She would not live a lie. She would not stay married for the kids and pretend. She would not have a "look-good" marriage. She would have God's promised, overabundant love and nothing short of it. Or she would have nothing.

Now this made sense. And it was the truth. *I thought,* Now, I can work with that.

In that moment and in an instant, I was all in. Nobody but nobody was going to turn up the heat and start cooking anything new with my wife but me.

Do you feel like your marriage is burnt to a crisp? Like you can't stand the sight of your spouse for one more second, let alone for the rest of your life?

Steve and I know exactly where you are. We're here to tell you there is hope.

This is not a book written for couples who want to make their good marriage even better, although we believe our "no-fail recipe for reviving your marriage" can do that too. This is not a book designed for those hoping to get married who want a head start on good advice they might need, although we think this book is packed with good advice that can help them too. This is not a book for those trying to get along better with their mother, siblings, or coworkers, although the relationship principles we've packed in here can help any relationship thrive.

> "Do you feel like your marriage is
> *burnt* to a crisp? We're here to
> tell you there is hope."

Finally, this is not a book written for a desperate spouse who wants to turn around a broken marriage when the other spouse doesn't. If the husband and wife are not willing to work together on this, our no-fail recipe will be a big flop. It takes determination and effort from both partners to turn desperate into something divine.

This *is* a book written specifically for the husband and wife who are so lonely and hurt in their marriage they feel like they're dying … and for the husbands and wives who are so angry they wish their spouse was. (You know who you are.) This is a book for two spouses whose marriage seems beyond fixing but they're both too stubborn to give up. It's for spouses who can agree that no matter how they feel or how complicated it's gotten, they'll both give it one more shot.

When we sat down to write this book, we were writing it for you. And we are praying for you, the desperate couples, the hopeless couples, the couples headed straight for divorce court. We want you to know if our marriage could radically change, yours can too. We promise.

You can have hope. You can find friendship, love, passion, and common goals again. I know that's almost impossible to believe from where you are right now, but Steve and I are living proof you can start again from scratch and cook up a whole new marriage relationship. One that is healthier for you, your spouse, and your kids. One that keeps your bank accounts from being handed over to lawyers and mediators. One that preserves your family legacy and traditions. One that shows your children what commitment truly means.

> "We want you to know if our marriage could radically change, *yours* can too."

It won't be easy at first. Your hearts have been trampled, your souls wounded. Your feelings may not line up with some of the things we're going to ask you to try, do, and say. But trust us when we say if you do these things, your marriage will change for the better. Sooner than you think.

When my husband and I talked that night more than a decade ago, we did not *feel* like staying together. Our hearts had hardened towards each other years before. We had lost our love and friendship. We did not even feel slightly affectionate. Shoot, we couldn't even talk civilly. Everything had been a fight for so long we were like two tigers suddenly let out of their cages, nosing around, growling, and even nipping at each other every time we came in close contact. The threat that we could rip each other to shreds any second was always right there.

We made a decision to start over not because we felt like it, but because we came to the conclusion it was the right thing to do. I can tell you our emotions did not fully line up with our decision that night. I can also tell you it didn't take long before our emotions started to realign. Hardened hearts can heal. Scar tissue can soften or fall away, leaving hearts open and tender toward each other again.

We encourage you to read each chapter in this book carefully and take our suggestions seriously. Starting today, put them into practice in your marriage. The sooner you both get on board and decide to begin again, the sooner you will enjoy the results of creating something together instead of eating alone.

"Hardened hearts can *heal*. Scar tissue can soften or fall away, leaving hearts open and tender toward each other again."

Today, Steve and I are each other's best friends. We trust each other, count on each other, and look forward to every minute together. We consider it a compliment when our now-grown children tell us to "get a room." We look forward to growing old together, traveling to see more of the world, and rocking grandbabies on a front porch someday. We have created a new love that grows deeper daily.

So grab your apron or chef coat and get ready to start again from scratch. A great marriage is waiting for you to pull it all together. Believe me, you too can transform your marriage from desperate to delicious.

When I told Laine we could start again from scratch, I meant it. We would do more than just improve the same tired dish. We would go all-in and create a totally new marriage. I told her somehow we would make it sizzle.

I finally understood that starting over was not giving in. It was getting everything I ever wanted. If my marriage ended, I would lose everything I had ever worked for. I would lose any money I had, my wife, and my kids. I would lose my sense of purpose. What would be the point of going to work every day if I was providing for no one but myself, building nothing for anyone but myself?

I finally understood that starting over was not giving in. It was *getting* everything I ever wanted.

It was a no-brainer for me because I knew it was going to give me everything I prayed for. How could I know that starting again from scratch would fix everything? Because if two people start over from scratch, there is no longer anything bad behind them or between them. The slate is wiped totally clean. All your issues disappear. In an instant, you start fresh. It's like a magic wand, I promise you. Twelve years ago, Laine and I made a commitment to start again from scratch. We started cooking up something totally new. Today, I am enjoying all of it, all day, every day, every bite of life.

Men, don't stay lost. Quit listening to your divorced friends. Get serious about this and get it fixed, just like you would anything else that needs to be fixed. Your wife is important. Man up and read every chapter. There are a lot of time-saving shortcuts here. I know you usually skip the instructions, put things together on your own, and hope whatever you're building turns out right. As I'm sure you've figured out by now, your marriage doesn't work that way. Right now, you need some quality ingredients and some good directions to get your marriage sizzling again instead of burnt beyond recognition. Those directions are in here.

Do it for your kids. Do it for your finances. Do it for your family name. Do it to have peace and joy and love in your life, maybe for the first time. Do it for yourself, so you can be childlike again, worry-free. Do what you want, when you want, maybe for the first time.

Do it so you can finally discover how tasty the right recipe for marriage can be.

Burnt to a Crisp: Our No-Fail Recipe

INGREDIENTS:

1 charred-beyond-recognition marriage

1 desperate, lonely wife

1 angry, checked-out husband

An agreement from both spouses to start again from scratch

An agreement from both spouses to read this book

DIRECTIONS:

Take the husband and wife and get them together at room temperature.

Have both spouses examine the mess that is their marriage. If either spouse gets heated, stop assembling the ingredients until everyone is back at room temperature. Have both spouses agree to start again from scratch. Shake on it. Make a spit pact. Double-dog dare each other.

Determine with everything you can muster you won't quit. Mix in a reading plan to get this book finished, individually or together, and let sit.

Burnt to a Crisp:
Our No-Fail Recipe Card

From the Kitchen of: _____

INGREDIENTS:

_____

_____

_____

_____

_____

_____

_____

DIRECTIONS:

_____

_____

_____

_____

_____

_____

_____

_____

_____

Burnt Butter Frosting

This recipe makes enough frosting for one 9x13-inch cake

Prep Time: 5 mins | Cook Time: 6 mins | Total Time: 11 mins

INGREDIENTS:

1/2 cup butter

4 cups confectioners' sugar

4 tablespoons milk

1 teaspoon vanilla extract

DIRECTIONS:

Place butter in a saucepan over medium-high heat. Cook, stirring constantly, until butter is a nice tan color. If it gets dark brown or black you have allowed it to burn too long.

When butter has been "burned," remove the saucepan from the heat. Slowly mix in confectioners' sugar and vanilla. Beat with an electric mixer on high speed until light and fluffy. Beat in the milk a tablespoon at a time until desired spreading consistency is achieved. Use immediately, as this frosting will set up quickly.

Burnt Butter Frosting

NOTE FROM LAINE AND STEVE:

We started with this recipe because we want you to know that sweetness in your marriage is just around the corner. Something beautiful can come out of something that looks burnt. We also chose only to give you the frosting recipe, not a cake to go with it, because it's not time yet to have your cake and eat it too. But that time is coming. We promise. Start cooking and it's coming soon.

NOTES:

_____

_____

_____

_____

_____

_____

_____

_____

_____

_____

_____

_____

The Secret Sauce

"Taste and see that the LORD is good.
Oh, the joys of those who take refuge in him!"
Psalm 34:8 (New Living Translation)

Some of you are groaning already. I can hear you. You just looked at the top of this page and thought, *Good grief, now they're going to preach at me. That's just what I don't need. They're going to tell me all we need is God and magically our marriage will be all better. Like that's gonna help.*

Not exactly.

We *are* going to make the case right up front here that without God in our lives and on our side, we could not have totally transformed our marriage the way we did. That's the truth. The two of us never could have done it by ourselves. Think about it. If Steve and I could have fixed our marriage, broken our cycle of fighting and bickering, don't you think we would have? We may have acted dumb a lot of the time, but we're not stupid.

Now, we're not telling you what to do. But I'd bet money you haven't been able to fix your marriage by yourselves either. Otherwise, you wouldn't have chosen this book, right? So bear with us. We want to give you what we believe are the very best ingredients for creating a marriage filled with love, joy, and peace again, or maybe for the first time ever. We would be doing you a huge disservice if we gave you the recipe for something great but left out the secret sauce that truly transforms it into a dish that's out of this world. We're talking a marriage that's like a five-star culinary experience. One you'll crave more and more of every day.

You can skip this chapter and go right for the rest of the book. You'll get tons of really great advice that can lead to some permanent positive changes in your marriage. You might even recreate a marriage that's a lot tastier than the one you've got now. Or you can read this chapter carefully, weigh the evidence of what happened in our lives, and decide for yourself if you want to try what we're calling the "Secret Sauce" that will make your marriage as fine as anything a winning Iron Chef could dish up.

If you're as down-and-out as we were, you'll dive right into this chapter and take it as seriously as the rest. Put every bit into practice as hard and fast as you can. When God becomes an integral part of your life recipe, it turns out better than anything you can cook up by yourself.

The verse at the beginning of this chapter says, "Taste and see that the Lord is good." That's a challenge and a promise from God to you, and I love it because right there in that one verse God shows He is an equal opportunity God who knows how to appeal to all His children. The right-brained creative people will enjoy "tasting" how good God is, while the left-brained logical people can "see" His goodness with their very own eyes. God says we can access His goodness through the rich experience of tasting. We can also prove His love to ourselves by observing what He does in our lives.

One more thing: Notice the way this verse is worded. Remember action verbs from way back in English class, probably around third or fourth grade? "Taste" and "see" are both action verbs. If you can stretch your memory a little bit further and recall the different kinds of sentences, you'll recognize this verse as an imperative sentence. It has that little old "understood You" as the subject. That makes it a command.

You taste … *You* see …

God is ordering us to taste and see His goodness. He is telling us to do something, and if we do there are promises He will fulfill for us. Like showing us His goodness and giving us joy when we take refuge in Him.

When we obey Him, He opens our eyes. Even in the midst of our troubles, we will be able to see His hand at work and taste (and smell, since smell is connected to our sense of taste) the sweetness of His presence. Maybe that sounds a little weird to you, or maybe that sounds too good to be true. (You) Do what God is telling you to do in this little imperative sentence and we guarantee you'll like the results.

Seriously, in the place you're in, what have you got to lose? Just sayin'.

I don't know where you are with God. Maybe you don't know Him at all and aren't sure you want to. Maybe you've heard about Him all your life but never really known Him personally. Maybe you were on personal speaking terms with God at one point in your life but can't seem to hear Him now.

Since this is a book called *Start Again from Scratch*, I'll take you back to the beginning of my relationship with God. I grew up in the South, and growing up Southern means growing up in church. I knew the stories of Noah and the Ark, David and Goliath, and the miracles Jesus performed. I even knew that Jesus loved me and died on the cross for my sins. I was just a kid when I prayed a prayer and asked Jesus into my heart.

When I grew up and got married, I still went to church. It's just what you do if you're a Mississippi girl married to a Mississippi boy and you live in the South. We didn't even limit our church-going to Sundays. We served in ministry and I sang in the choir. Steve and I might fight late into the night on Saturday, but our family would be polished and planted in the pew to learn more about Jesus on Sunday morning. That was exactly our problem. We knew all *about* Jesus, but we never got to *know* Jesus.

I never heard the word "grace" until I was in my 30s. Most of my life I thought God was about a lot of rules. I condemned myself a lot. I thought if I wasn't perfect I was never gonna get to heaven.

It's tough to develop a personal relationship with someone you are afraid of, one you think you are not good enough for, that you never talk to or spend time with. For Steve and me, this was a big part of our problem with each other, and it was definitely our problem with God. Our relationship with God and with each other had dried up completely because we didn't understand grace. We just did not put much into getting to know God because we didn't expect to get anything out of it. Being married and going to church were just what we did, not what we wanted to do.

Yes, I took my family to church for years. But it took my father dying and my marriage almost coming to an end for me to develop a real, personal relationship with God. When I came to the end of myself, that is when I really started talking to God. I had been working so hard for so long, but nothing was turning out right. I still had no real money or security. I really had no wife. My family was suffering.

Not long before Laine and I began to revive our marriage, my father-in-law came to see me. We walked out of the garage office where I was living and walked onto the driveway. I no longer knew what to do or how to fix any of it. Was I a fool kicking a dead horse or a genius, persistent and determined to keep the course, despite everyone's counsel to quit? It was a very fine line between the two. But one thing God gave you creates an advantage. Only you determine when the game is over.

I had about fifteen credit cards. Got them in the mail on a Saturday, and they had zero percent interest for twelve months. I had taken cash advances to cover the short months, to pay for the kids' private school, my office equipment, and now, whatever needed it, even the other credit cards. The bank had cut off my unsecured line of credit, stating that they saw little earning power in me or my companies. My accountant was urging me to file bankruptcy, and my marriage was in a worse state than my finances.

Now Laine's father looked me straight in the eyes and said, "Steve, I know it's bad. But tell me how bad it really is."

I said, "Do you remember when I asked you seventeen years ago if I could marry your daughter? You said, 'I'll tell you what. You can marry her, Steve, but if you ever get divorced I will shoot your feet off with my shotgun. You might divorce my daughter, but you will have to continue the remainder of your little life without any feet.' Now you are asking me how bad it is. Well, for the past three months, I have been thinking that I could probably do okay in life without any feet. I have given all my efforts and made three hard runs at the oil business and haven't made it. And I think I might rather live with the devil himself than live with your daughter another day. I have decided to make one more run at the oil business for one more year and if it doesn't work I am going back into the construction business."

Laine's father seemed to think that was reasonable. Then I asked this man who had been happily married for a very long time what I should do about my marriage to his daughter, and I found that he had little advice. I guess even he thought we were beyond repair. Or maybe I just didn't understand.

So there I was on a beautiful Saturday afternoon, beyond broke and utterly lost for direction. Laine was watching the kids splash and play in the backyard pool, and I felt so far away from all of them. I knew if I walked back there, my wife would glare at me with hate-filled eyes silently screaming "Loser." I couldn't even enjoy a good relationship with my kids, because every time Laine protected them from the truth of how bad our relationship was, it felt like she was just shielding them from me.

I walked back to my live-in garage office, so depressed and desperate all I wanted to do was hide and find a minute of comfort. I knew that my scornful wife would march in shortly to confront me. She would reprimand me for resting in the garage instead of playing with my kids. I was nothing. After forty years of back-breaking effort, all I had on the entire planet was a few computers, some files, and a creaking couch in a small space in a dark, lonely garage. A seven-foot couch that marked a seven-foot space for me, the only seven feet that kept the universe from collapsing in on me. This is all my hard work and honesty had gotten me? A seven-foot space of isolation? In other words...hell.

What had I done wrong? How could I endure this pain? Why didn't hard work and honesty and integrity pay off? How could my own wife hate me? How could she threaten to take everything from me? Didn't she know me? How could she laugh in derision at me? Didn't she know me at all?

I lay down on the couch in the dark, hoping not to hear her footsteps, praying not to be seen, begging God to stop the pain.

I literally cried out, "Help me, God. I don't know what to do. Tell me what to do. Please, God, tell me what to do!" I broke down in choking sobs, screaming out loud. "God, please slap me with your instructions because I can't hear you. Have I ever heard you? Do you even exist? Slap me hard, God, because if I miss your voice and instruction this time, well, I am out of time." The sounds coming out of me and the darkness in my heart felt like the depths of hell.

And that's where I begged God to come rescue me. I asked Him to storm the gates of hell and pull me out. I asked the God who created the whole universe to step down from Heaven and pull me out of the hell of my own making. "God, I know you're busy and all, but could you drop everything you're doing and come to hell on purpose and in person to get me? Because I don't like it here anymore. I know you told me not to come here a few million times and I didn't listen. But could I interrupt all your big, important business so you could make me your child again?"

Now I see it took years for me to descend into hell. My whole life really. My heart had been bruised and battered by a bully here, a broken heart there. I learned to fake like I didn't care until I convinced myself I really didn't. A few lies, my parents' divorce, a few beers, a few girlfriends, a few more beers, I learned to cover the pain by doing everything on my own. No one cared, so no one should get too close. Not my wife, not even God. I would do it myself. So I did, but look where it had gotten me. Facedown on an old couch, screaming in agony for God to make it all stop. When I told God to slap me hard so I could hear Him, this time He took me up on it.

My friends had told me to start doctoring my files in case Laine left, so I could make out better in our divorce. I pulled out those files and stared at them. Keep going down the path of pain? Or shred them and get honest with my wife? It was an age-old choice between good and evil.

When Laine came to me, I chose to show her all the debt and the mess and the mistakes. I told my wife that she shouldn't leave now, because if she did she would be walking away owing half of the $600 thousand debt we had. I said she should stay one more year because I thought what I was working on would work. If not, she could leave then. A truly honest and unselfish act. But to do it,

I had to let go of Plan B, which included letting go of anything that would put me in a better position if we divorced. You can't go all-in to save your marriage if you are planning your divorce strategy on the side. If you are preserving and doing the things you've lined up for Plan B, you cannot accomplish the things in Plan A.

Laine responded by telling me she was done with our old life. She wanted to get out of hell too. Together, we finally understood we could not do this by ourselves. Together, we had to let God do something with our marriage and our mess. That's the beauty of the end-of-the-line crisis. There is nothing left for you to do. You have to let go and let God get his hands on it. It's a relief, actually. When there's nothing left, that's a great place for Him to work. And a great place for you to start over. It's also where the devil becomes visible. He is greedy and although it feels like he has everything else, he demands to take the one thing you have left. Your marriage. But in this move, he becomes obvious.

Did I want to start over? Heck, no. I'd put in seventeen years of hard work with no results. Start over? Are you crazy? But if my marriage failed, then the years of hard work were a total waste. What was there to gain by giving up, by quitting? I could have revenge, sure. I could put all the worst credit debt in her name, maybe. Whoopee! Then I would be a millionaire, right? Hardly. I would only have to support myself. That would be easier. Not. She would become a lifelong adversary sent directly from satan himself. And she would have my kids. Now I would have double the problems.

When Laine and I agreed to start over, I realized suddenly I truly had been married to the devil. Not Laine. Don't get me wrong here. She was not the devil. My marriage was not the devil. The devil was the devil, and while we had spent seventeen years working hard, so had he. He had spent all those years working his way into our marriage until all we could see when we looked at each other was him. Every time we faced each other with anger, every time we fought, it was him. Every time we thought or said ugly words, we saw the devil in each other. Every time we turned a cold shoulder or walked out on each other's pain, the devil had a field day. It took us all those years to turn and kneel side-by-side so together we could face the devil and kick him to the curb.

Our marriage was not the problem. It was the solution. We had lost everything else. And it was all so blinding. For a long time, we believed that if we dumped our marriage too, that would fix everything. But the marriage was all we had left. And it was from God. Why would we want to destroy the one thing we had? How would that possibly fix anything? We had to realize it was the only good thing left and the only thing that could be used as the cornerstone to build our new life upon. That's when we could see the devil's lie for what it was.

"Our marriage was not the problem. It was the *solution*."

When Laine and I decided to start again from scratch, the first thing we did was drop to our knees. We talked out loud to God, asking Him to forgive us for the way we had ignored Him and each other. Maybe this will be hard for you. It was for me. But realize before you start that your only audience is your wife and God. And they are both on your side. They are for you. Knowing that, there is nothing to fear. They will both love you for what you say. They will take joy in the childlike innocence of inexperienced prayer. That is what God lives for, you know.

We acknowledged that we wanted Him involved in every part of our lives, especially our marriage. We wanted Him to guide us to be better parents, help us to love each other again. We told Him we would talk more often to Him, learn more of what He had to say to us in His book (the Bible) and put Him first in our marriage. When we said "Amen" at the end of that prayer, I promise you peace entered our home. Peace like we hadn't experienced in years. Suddenly, we got a little taste and a small glimpse that God is good. We took refuge in Him, trusting that He would help us find our way to joy.

We knew there was still lots of hard stuff to come. Lots to talk through and work out. We had spent years developing bad habits and poor communication, and those would not just vanish overnight. Still, there was a feeling of peace. Prayer planted a small seed of hope in our hearts. We got up from our knees and knew. Something was different. We would be unstoppable.

Steve and I believe God created marriage to be a covenant not between two beings, but between three: a husband, a wife, and God. Dictionary.com says the word *covenant* means "agreement" and was originally from the Latin *convenire*, which means to "come together." In the Bible, a covenant was an agreement between God and his people. In a covenant, God promises His people something and usually requires something from them in return. He gives and we give.

It's a two-way street, but guess who gets the better end of the deal? The creator of the world who owns absolutely everything, is all-powerful and offers us eternity? Or the human beings whose lives are finite and whose offerings back to God consist of a lot of begging for what we want, a ton of brokenness and sin, and a bunch of cries for help? *Hint:* We won the lottery on this one.

In the Old Testament, God made covenants with Noah (never to flood the earth again), Abraham (that he would be the father of nations), and Moses (that he would lead the Israelites to the Promised Land). In the New Testament, God makes a covenant through Jesus Christ with all people—every single man, woman and child—that if we believe in Jesus, we will be saved.

When a husband and wife say their marriage vows, they are making a covenant not only with each other but also with God. Marriage is the joining together of all the aspects of God. The Bible says that people were created in God's image.

> "So God created mankind in his own image, in the image of God he created them; male and female he created them."—Genesis 1:27 (NEW INTERNATIONAL VERSION)

When a marriage is formed, two people become one. When they have a personal relationship with Christ and include Him in it, the three become one and display all God's glory. All the male characteristics of God and all the female characteristics of God come together in the union of marriage to give us a glimpse of the fullness of God in all His glory.

See, God created me to be Laine Lawson Craft. He created me to be a woman who is spunky and energetic. He created me to be a talker and a doer. He created me to help women heal from their hurts and hangups. He created me to like to cook. I'm sometimes called the "Paula Deen of ministry," and I take that as a compliment. God has certain jobs He created Laine to do.

God created my husband to be Steve Craft. Steve is not like Laine. God created my man Steve to be a scientist, a geologist. He created Steve with a great work ethic. He created Steve to keep trying and not give up when things are tough. God has certain jobs He created Steve to do.

We believe God also created our marriage. Together, we are the Crafts. Our marriage is a third entity. It has its own characteristics and unique jobs to do. Through the story of our marriage, we can help other marriages heal. Through our legacy of togetherness, we can show other couples the benefits of lifetime commitment. Through living a great marriage, we can show the world what God looks like.

Marriage is like a three-legged stool. If you remove God or never bother to include Him in the first place, your stool is going to be missing a leg. A three-legged stool can't stand on two legs. It falls over and can't get up. It's pretty much useless. Without God, our marriage is just a two-legged stool. It's Laine and Steve butting heads together, jostling for position, and getting frustrated over our differences.

Marriage with God stands up under pressure. With all three legs, we can appreciate the part each leg plays. Instead of our differences making us crazy, with God we can appreciate how we complement each other as different parts of His image.

If you have never gotten to know the God of the Bible personally, now is the perfect time. You can start by getting a Bible, pulling one up online or going to a Bible-teaching church. You can learn what Jesus did for you by reading the book of John in the New Testament. Then turn to Romans next to read what Jesus' death on the cross means for you and for your spouse.

The Bible tells the most romantic love story of all. It is the story of a God who created a beautiful world with people He loved with all His heart as His amazing children. Then that perfect world became corrupt with sin and evil. The children He created turned away from Him and broke His heart. Still, He loved them so much He sent His son Jesus Christ to become a man, fully God but also fully partaking in the human experience from birth to death.

Jesus came to earth to sacrifice Himself by dying a brutal death nailed to a cross so that evil would not win. Jesus is the ultimate superhero. He overcame death by coming back to life after three days in a tomb. He died and rose again to save anyone who would believe in Him.

Jesus removed the barrier between sinful men and a righteous God, allowing man the freedom to have a personal relationship again with his creator, his loving father. The Bible says all He requires in return is that we believe He is God, that He died for our sins and rose again. If we confess we are sinners and ask for forgiveness, God's mercy and grace restore our relationship with Him in an instant. We are given eternal life in Heaven and the Holy Spirit to counsel us and comfort us here on earth.

> "For God so loved the world, that he gave his only begotten Son, that whosoever believeth in him should not perish, but have everlasting life."
> —John 3:16 (KING JAMES VERSION)

> "If we confess our sins, he will forgive our sins, because we can trust God to do what is right. He will cleanse us from all the wrongs we have done."
> —1 John 1:9 (NEW CENTURY VERSION)

That is what Steve and I got when we knelt down and prayed. We confessed our sins. We believed God was who He said He was. We believed He was a good God who would help us. He would come to our rescue. We could taste and see that He is good, and we could run to Him to be our refuge, our safe place. Once we did, He kept His end of the bargain. As 1 John 1:9 says, He cleansed us from all the things we had done wrong. In an instant, the gunk we had packed in our hearts for years was scooped out and thrown away.

Gone.

Poof.

Ezekiel 36:26 (NLT) says it this way:

> "And I will give you a new heart, and I will put a new spirit in you. I will take out your stony, stubborn heart and give you a tender, responsive heart."

That's exactly what happened when we stopped aiming at each other and turned our attention to God. Just like that, we were ready to start again from scratch.

The Secret Sauce: Our No-Fail Recipe

INGREDIENTS:

1 willing-to-try husband

1 what-have-we-got-to-lose wife

2 pairs of knees

2 bowed heads

2 sorry hearts

1 forgiving God

1 Bible (and any tools you need to understand it)

DIRECTIONS:

Take the husband and wife and have them bend down on the two pairs of knees. Add two bowed heads.

Mix in the confessions of two sorry hearts willing to admit the things they have done wrong and to ask God to help them start over. Fold in the forgiveness of God.

Let the forgiveness marinate. Add Bible reading and let bake.

The Secret Sauce: Taste and See

*I*f you have never prayed to God before or it has been so long that you have no idea what to say, you can repeat something like this:

Dear Jesus,

I just want to say I'm sorry. I am sorry for the ugly ways I have behaved toward my husband/wife. I am sorry for my disrespect and unloving heart toward the spouse you created for me. Please forgive me for all the things I have said and done that injured my spouse and hurt your heart. Please forgive me for all my sins against you and against my mate. I want to start again from scratch with you in our marriage. Please, Jesus, come into our hearts and clean them out. We believe that you died on the cross for our sins. We believe that you rose again and if we confess this from our mouths you promise to save us from those sins. Thank you for dying for us. Thank you for giving us marriage. Now please help me to forgive my spouse. Help me to love my spouse. Help me to follow you all the days of my life.

In Jesus' name I pray, Amen.

When you pray this prayer, you are entering into the covenant of marriage the way we believe it was meant to be. You are starting a new relationship with God and with your spouse, and it will take daily nurturing to flourish. From here on out, you need to talk to God and read His love letter to you (the Bible) every day. Multiple times a day. It's not as hard as you think to make God the best habit in your life. You can talk to Him anywhere. In the shower. In the car. In your bed. Kneeling beside your bed.

Praying together with your spouse for just a few minutes when you start and end your day will radically improve your relationship with God and each other. It may feel awkward at first if you have never prayed together beyond a quick blessing of the food, but you will quickly come to look forward to these special times together.

Thank Him for what He is doing in your lives, share with him any concerns and requests, and praise Him for the blessings He has already given you. If you do not wake or go to bed at the same times, set aside a few minutes once or twice a day to pray together. If your jobs frequently keep you apart, set prayer "dates" by phone, Skype or FaceTime.

In your personal relationship with God, try talking to Him as you first wake up and as you drift off to sleep. Start and end your day with Him. Seek His guidance throughout the day. Get used to asking Him what He wants you to do before you make decisions. Soon, you will recognize His voice in your spirit.

Get a version of the Bible you can understand and begin to read it every day. The Bible is packed full of promises from God to us. God wants to bless your socks off when you serve Him with all your heart. Here are just a few of the things He says:

> "Trust in the Lord with all your heart; do not depend on your own understanding. Seek his will in all you do, and he will show you which path to take."—Proverbs 3:5-6 (NLT)

> "Look at the birds. They don't plant or harvest or store food in barns, for your heavenly Father feeds them. And aren't you far more valuable to him than they are?"—Matthew 6:26 (NLT)

> "Worship the LORD your God, and his blessing will be on your food and water. I will take away sickness from among you."—Exodus 23:25 (NIV)

"But my God shall supply all your need according to his riches in glory by Christ Jesus."
—Philippians 4:19 (KJV)

"When people live so that they please the Lord, even their enemies will make peace with them."
—Proverbs 16:7 (NCV)

"Call to me in times of trouble. I will save you, and you will honor me."—Psalm 50:15 (NCV)

Who wouldn't want to get to know a God who promises all that and much, much more! In the New Testament, Jesus ate a meal with His disciples we know as the Last Supper. During their meal, he took a loaf of bread, broke it in half and told them it was His body, which was broken for them. John 6:51 says, "I am the living bread that came down from heaven. Whoever eats this bread will live forever." (NIV)

"Call to me in times of *trouble*.
I will save you, and you will honor me."
—Psalm 50:15 (NCV)"

The Bible contains the words Jesus said, the promises God makes to us, and practical guidance for daily living. It is full of wisdom that still applies to our lives in the post-modern twenty-first century and beyond. Read it every day, and you will discover new meaning in passages you may have read a hundred times. You will find verses you have never seen before. And you will get to know Jesus as the best friend who is closer than a brother (Proverbs 18:24). Daily Bible reading provides nourishment for your soul.

If you don't have a Bible or don't understand what you are reading, you can go online and find tons of sermon notes, Scripture applications, devotionals, and more. You can also go to a local Christian bookstore and look at different versions and translations. Ask the employees if they can explain to you the differences and features. A good study Bible contains dictionaries, maps, commentaries and other helps for you to gain more context and comprehension as you read.

If you find reading a hard habit to form on your own, you can sign up online for Bible readings to be emailed to you daily. You can also listen to an audio Bible in your car or on your computer. There are many one-year reading plans and one-year Bibles that assign daily readings to you so you can finish the entire Bible in one year by reading about ten minutes each day.

Just one caution: God is not an ATM or slot machine God. He does not grant every wish like a genie from a bottle. In fact, it may seem like things get a little worse before they get better. Or it may get better at first, then you may face a setback. Don't worry. God is still there. He's still listening. He wants you to keep calling on Him.

God loves you, your spouse, and your marriage more than anyone ever could. He knows every hair on your head. He knows the number of your days. He has plans and a future for you, and they are good. *If* you believe in Him. *If* you start living your days with Him. *If* you start living *for* Him.

A couple who begins to develop or strengthen a personal relationship with God the Father, Jesus Christ, and the Holy Spirit adds a very special Secret Sauce to their marriage. God loves you unconditionally, Jesus died to save you, and the Holy Spirit lives in those who have invited Him in to give them wisdom, comfort them and counsel them. If you acknowledge God (and by God we mean the Trinity, the three-in-one) and hand the control of your marriage to Him, He will give you grace and mercy. He can teach two people starving for attention and affection how to create a feast of love again. He can make your marriage a living miracle.

The Secret Sauce:
Our No-Fail Recipe Card

From the Kitchen of: _____

INGREDIENTS:

_____

_____

_____

_____

_____

_____

_____

DIRECTIONS:

_____

_____

_____

_____

_____

_____

_____

_____

_____

Homemade Bread
Makes 2 loaves

INGREDIENTS:

5 cups white all-purpose flour, divided

2 tablespoons yeast

2 tablespoons sugar

1 teaspoon salt

2 cups warm water

1/4 cup cooking oil

DIRECTIONS:

Place 4 cups of the flour into a large bowl. Add yeast, sugar and salt, and stir. Pour in hot water and oil and mix until well combined—it will be sticky.

Add remaining 1 cup flour in increments until dough is no longer sticky. Knead about 5 minutes until dough is elastic and smooth. Place dough back into bowl and cover with a damp tea towel. Let dough rise until double in size, about 1/2 hour.

Punch dough down and divide in half. Shape each half of dough to fit into a well-oiled loaf pan and leave to rise until dough has reached the rim of the pan. Bake at 400 degrees for 40 minutes.

Rub hot loaves with water and wrap in a teatowel to 'sweat' to soften the crust.

Homemade Bread

NOTE FROM LAINE AND STEVE:

We chose this recipe because the bread would not turn out just right without the yeast. Yeast is the secret ingredient to make the bread rise, just like God is the secret sauce to make our marriages just right.

NOTES:

_____

_____

_____

_____

_____

_____

_____

_____

_____

_____

_____

_____

_____

_____

_____

Ingredients

*"Simple ingredients, treated with respect ...
put them together and you will always
have a great dish."*
Jose Andres Puerta

Fresh, Quality Flavor

Forgiveness

"Forgiveness is the oil that love cooks in."
Ron Moore

When I decided to become college roommates with a girlfriend from high school, I had no idea it would affect the rest of my life. Suzanne and I only shared a room for one semester, but it was enough to set the course for my future. Suzanne transferred to another university after that short time as roomies, and we didn't stay in touch for a long time. Then about two-and-a-half years later Suzanne called me out of the blue. We were both back in our home-town for the summer, and she asked me if I wanted to go with her to a Commodores concert at the Coliseum that weekend.

Lionel Richie? Absolutely. Sign me up, I thought.

When I headed over to Suzanne's house the night of the concert, I noticed a really good-looking guy standing by the back door. Since I am ever the shy, quiet type (Not!), I walked right up to him with a big smile and said, "Hey, I'm Laine." (Great opening line, right?)

He said, "I'm Steve." (Now the conversation was really rolling.)

Whoa. Wait just a minute! I thought. *Steve? As in, Suzanne's big brother Steve? The one I never even noticed in high school? This is Suzanne's brother Steve?*

Then I uttered a single, fateful sentence that would set a whole lot in motion.

"You should come with us," I said.

When Steve started to shake his head no, I quickly transitioned to full-on flirt mode.

"What, you'd rather stay home with your momma than come out and have a great time with me and your sister?" I teased.

I don't know if it was my flirting, my outgoing personality, my blonde cuteness, or just the challenge itself that got Steve off the back steps and into the car, but it didn't really matter because soon the three of us were on our way to hear the Commodores.

Or maybe Suzanne heard the Commodores.

I'm not sure Steve and I heard much more than our own heartbeats and our voices trying to connect with each other over the music. The attraction was instant and powerful. From that night on, we were a couple. I gotta admit, Suzanne was miffed. I'm sure she thought it was gross to see her former high school girlfriend kissing her big brother.

Only six weeks later, I confided to my former roomie, "I think your brother is going to be my husband."

"No way," Suzanne replied. "Y'all are much too different. There is *no way* that would work."

Two years later, in May of 1987, Steve and I tied the knot in my parents' backyard.

Suzanne was right on the money that Steve and I were very different, and her dire prediction that we were too different to make it work almost came true. Like many couples, our differences initially attracted us to each other. Steve was fascinated by how high-energy, passionate, raw, and real I was. I loved his quiet steadiness and scientific way of thinking. He could sit down and do test papers all day and like it. Yuck! After we were married for a short time, however, these differences quickly became major sources of friction.

Steve's quieter way of doing things meant he didn't dote on me, praise me. He didn't want to be the life of the party. He wasn't lovey-dovey and affectionate. He was basically a lot like the old marriage joke that goes, "Honey, I told you once at the beginning of our relationship that I love you. If that ever changes, I'll let you know."

"Like many couples, our differences initially *attracted* us to each other."

My loud boldness made him tune out and shut down. The more I poked and prodded with my words, trying to get Steve to come out of his shell, the more he was like a turtle who pulled himself as far inside as he could. When you combine two very different personalities with two different sets of expectations and mix in a lot of challenging circumstances that come up during marriage, it's a recipe for disaster if you don't know how to turn your differences into devotion.

From the early years of our marriage, it was very challenging. We were both self-employed, so we never had a paycheck we could count on. I had two miscarriages. Then we had three children in three years. Our third child, our only daughter, was born septic and spent some of her first year in an oxygen tent. Many times we did not know if she would live or die.

There were a lot of trials and tribulations right off the bat. Life got painful very quickly. And since we didn't really have a personal relationship with God, we didn't have anything to lean on but ourselves.

I fell in love with Laine because she was cute and sexy and fun to be around. At first, she looked at me like I hung the moon, like I did everything just right. But soon after we were married, when we never had enough money and all we did was work, she began looking at me like I couldn't do anything right. Then it seemed like she was always telling me I couldn't do anything right. Even when she didn't say those exact words, her facial expressions, tone of voice, and body language told me loud and clear what a worthless jerk I had become in her eyes.

She complained because I worked too hard and was gone all the time. I didn't want to hear it so I worked harder and left more. We both had strong work ethics and strong personalities, and we began keeping mental lists of who was working harder, doing more. I was determined to win, and Laine was determined to win. We never realized that for one of us to win meant the other one, the very person we were supposed to love more than ourselves, would have to lose. One ultimate winner in the end meant our marriage would have to lose. But we just couldn't see what we were doing to each other.

In my career, I had followed in my father's footsteps and become a geologist, trying to figure out where oil remained, looking for oil, raising money, looking for oil again. It's a high-pressure, high-stakes career, usually with more failure than success. Each prospect and attempt is like forming an entirely new business with a new project, new contracts, new capital, new work. And over the first seventeen years of our marriage, I accomplished about forty of these new projects. They were good projects. I knew this, as most were sold, in part, to larger oil companies. You might think that after forty tries, success would be assured. But it was not.

Laine started her own advertising company, and we struggled all the time to make ends meet. Laine lost two babies in the first few years of our marriage. Then we had our three kids back-to-back, and our daughter was born very sick. There was pressure building on all fronts. Circumstances were tough, but we made them far tougher by refusing to become a team. We thought we were each working hard to keep our family together, but we were really tearing each other apart.

> ## "Circumstances were tough, but we made them far tougher by *refusing* to become a team."

I think one of the lowest points for me came when my Dad was dying. Our three children were real young, and I took my two sons to visit their grandfather one last time at his home on the top of Lookout Mountain in Tennessee. It was hard. My sons hardly recognized him. The morning after we arrived, Dad and I took the boys down to watch the hang gliders take off from the mountaintop. It was a beautiful day, but before we even got to see the first glider soar my father's wife came outside and handed me a phone. Laine was on the other end, informing me that back home my office building had caught fire. I fell to my knees, rocked to the core. My marriage was a mess, my father was dying, and now everything I had worked for all my adult years was burning. And I could not fix any of it. My dad was in front of me and heard what was happening, and he began crying. My two little kids were behind me. I was the middle of this generational family sandwich, picturing everything I had worked for go up in flames.

My father and I knew. Now it was my turn to be the man, to lead.

Now? You have got to be kidding me. *I was kneeling on a mountaintop, facing my own mountain. "Okay, Steve, it's your turn now. You have lost everything. There is nothing left. But now you get to take over. And take care of everyone."*

Dad and I knew our brief time on the mountaintop was over before it had even gotten started.

I said goodbye to my father and drove the six hours home to see if anything was left, trying not to let my boys see me cry, not knowing what I would find when I got there. The office building held all the geological maps my father had given me when I took over the business, all the potential promising sites for striking oil. If they burned, my business was done. I prayed for God's will to be done. I told him that if the office was gone, I would get back into construction. If it remained, I would continue on. There was nothing I could do to stop my father from dying, nothing I could do to put out that fire.

When I got home, almost everything was gone. Everything except the maps I needed to keep working. But I had to find new office space. The owner of the building was in no hurry to repair the offices.

My marriage to Laine continued to spiral down as I mourned my father's death. I felt like she nagged me all the time. I responded in anger with ugly words and accusations. The layers of resentment built higher and higher until we lived in opposite ends of the house. Then I turned the garage into my office space and slept in it too. I began to consider leaving. Maybe I would move to Texas, a single man, and start over.

While Steve battled inner demons over his father's death and his fears of failure in business, I grew angry at his lack of attention to me and our marriage. It was hard taking care of three little children, maintaining a house, and working fifty- or sixty-hour weeks. I was flat-out exhausted all the time. On top of everything else, our precious daughter Kaylee had her many medical scares. All this pressure should have pushed me and Steve together to our knees. Instead, it kept pulling us apart.

I started finding solace in my friends and coworkers. We would head out to restaurants for a nice meal and a glass of wine after work. Looking back, I can see that going out was a cry for Steve's attention. It wasn't that those friends were so fun. It was that I wanted my husband to notice how often I was walking out the door. Deep down, I hoped every time that he would stop me or say he was going with me. I just wanted him to want to be with me. But he never did. I thought he didn't care what I did. So I dressed myself up and marched out our front door, a smile on my face but dying inside because my own husband didn't want to be with me.

Soon, my hurt turned to bitterness. How could Steve just send me out to have fun with everyone but him all the time? Would he care at all if another man hit on me? I was still young. I wanted to feel pretty. I needed to feel wanted. I felt I could never get that from Steve. After a while, I convinced myself if he didn't care I wouldn't either. Not caring was definitely better than hurting. My girlfriend and I called Steve "the meanest man on the planet." I'm ashamed to admit it now, but back then it got to the point where I loved to hate my husband. Isn't that terrible? I mean it. I loved to hate Steve.

Can you relate to any part of our story? Maybe the roots of bitterness have grown so deep in your marriage you don't think they can ever be yanked out. We're here to tell you they can, if you combine the key ingredients in this book and get them cooking in your life starting today.

One of the most vital ingredients is forgiveness. When you throw a heaping cup of forgiveness into the pot of your marriage, a miracle occurs. We're not kidding.

We know, we know, it's incredibly difficult to humble yourself and admit there are things you need to be forgiven for in your marriage, especially when you think of your spouse as the main bad guy. It's also a really tall order to forgive your spouse when they've done absolutely nothing to deserve to be forgiven.

We're here to tell you it doesn't matter whether you *want* to ask for forgiveness or *feel* like giving it. You simply can't move forward without it. Forgiveness is the key ingredient that determines the flavor of the rest of your marriage. Forgiveness is vital to cooking up a whole new life.

> **"Forgiveness is the key ingredient that determines the *flavor* of the rest of your marriage."**

Here are some of the reasons why forgiveness works: Asking for forgiveness requires humility. It is an act of moving toward your spouse, after all this time you've spent moving away. It's scary, because you don't know if your spouse will accept your offer. At first, rejection may be a real possibility. But Steve and I believe it is well worth every bit of the risk.

You have to say more than "I'm sorry" and ask the question "Will you forgive me?" Why? Because extending an "I'm sorry" means you are still in the driver's seat. You don't have to mean it, and it requires nothing from the one you are saying it to. When you say "Will you forgive me?" it takes you to a different level. Not only do you give up the control to the one you've hurt, but also they get put in the hot seat of making the right choice to accept your request and extend that forgiveness. If they don't right away, you'll still feel better knowing you did the right thing and you are now free.

This process of asking for and extending forgiveness in marriage packs a triple whammy: 1) You get to give your spouse a fresh start, 2) You get to receive a fresh start from your spouse, and 3) You both get released from the anger and bitterness you've been carrying. Forgiveness is the wonder drug of emotional dieting in marriage. One good dose and you drop hundreds of negative emotional pounds. Everyone who sees you will start telling you how good you look!

How do you do it? How do you forgive when you don't want to? When it is not fair? When you have every right to stay angry and resentful of the things your spouse has done to you, the words they have said to you, the wounds they have inflicted on your heart?

First, you pour some of that Secret Sauce from Chapter Two all over your hurting hearts 'til it marinates real deep all up in them. Then you make up your minds to just do it. Don't wait until you feel like it. When you have reached the boiling point in your marriage, that day may never come.

Forgiveness flows in two directions, vertically and horizontally. Vertical forgiveness is between you and God. Horizontal forgiveness takes place between you and your spouse.

Start vertically, so forgiveness flows between you and your Creator. Remember, being in right relationship with God is that Secret Sauce covering everything and making it all taste better. We highly recommend you first ask God to forgive you for the way you have treated your wife or your husband. Your spouse was a gift from God to you. You have taken that gift and broken it, forgotten it, or wished for a better gift. Tell God you are sorry for not appreciating your unique gift He picked especially for you.

When you ask God for forgiveness, He responds immediately. Your circumstances will not have changed one bit, but you will get an instant sense of peace, a glimmer of hope that floods your soul.

Say, "I am sorry, God, for the way I treated my husband/wife. I know you gave my spouse to me to be a partner for life. I have not honored you or my spouse in my words and actions. Will you forgive me and help me do better?"

Once you've gotten the vertical connection, it's time to get horizontal. Not that kind of horizontal, although it may come as soon as you get that fresh flavor of forgiveness. For this chapter we mean the horizontal forgiveness that takes place person-to-person, between husband and wife. The best time to start is now. Don't waste another minute in misery when you could be starting again from scratch. Choose to forgive even if you do not feel it. Then make it a daily decision.

Ask God to help you forgive. Say something like, "Will you help me forgive my spouse for all the wrongs they have done to me?" (Okay, I've got to share a quick funny with you. As I was typing that last sentence, autocorrect inserted "louse" instead of "spouse." I'm not kidding. So either way works. Ask God to help you forgive your "louse" or your "spouse." He'll get your point.) Once you've asked God to help you do it, it's time to face your spouse.

For Steve and me, the first act of forgiveness was confessing to each other all our mistakes, all our anger, all the ways we had wronged each other. That was the key. Once it was all in the open so there was nothing hidden, nothing fake, no lies between us, we spoke out loud our forgiveness. We knelt down arm-in-arm in our home and told God and each other how sorry we were. We told Him we would attempt to put the past in the past and start again from scratch.

When I told Steve all the things I had done, all the ugly words I had thought and said about him, all the ways I had hurt him, then I got to see and hear my husband truly extend grace to me and totally forgive me. I promise you, that felt like I got a taste of heaven right here on earth. It felt so good for my heart to be fresh and clean, to stand before my husband as his bride again.

You may think you are giving something when you ask for or extend forgiveness, but you are really getting a glimpse of what Heaven is going to be like when we stand face-to-face with our Maker and He forgives us and welcomes us into eternity.

Men, you won't even hardly understand what I am fixing to tell you. It can only be called a miracle. You probably won't believe it until it happens to you. When Laine and I got up from our knees after confessing and forgiving, something amazing happened. We could both feel the transformation already taking place. We could look into each other's eyes again and see hope instead of condemnation. We could smile at each other for the first time in a very long time.

We threw out the whole burnt-up mess we had made of our marriage and started creating a brand new recipe. The vital ingredient of forgiveness added a fantastic flavor. It was the secret super ingredient. It fixed the entire mess.

> **"We threw out the whole burnt-up mess we had made of our marriage and started *creating* a brand new recipe."**

Husbands, I promise you when you put confession, forgiveness, and grace into the recipe of your marriage, suddenly your wife is beautiful to you again because she accepted your forgiveness and she turned around and gave the same to you. In an instant, Laine went from being someone who was going to take everything away from me to the one who could give me back everything I had worked for, everything I ever wanted.

What you are doing by not forgiving and not confessing and not granting grace is living in fear. Fear is a tool of the devil. The Bible says to ask and you shall receive. So we ask God to fix our marriage and He says, "Okay, all you have to do is forgive her." Too often, we say, "Sorry, God. Can't do that. Anything but that. I need to hold onto those things that I have pending against her." Your list of things against her that are so important because surely some divorce judge will want proof of how awful she is. Wrong. If you head down that path, they won't even look. No one cares about your list. Your list is more worthless than worthless. Her list is too. In fact, I think "the list" may be the ultimate sin in marriage. Lists of grudges, wrongdoings, faults are kept for your control. Kept for revenge. Kept for future use in a pending divorce to destroy. Is it any wonder why your marriage is not working?

God gave us two things. He gave us His life force and He gave us freedom. Sure, you find safety and control by holding onto those things you have pending against her. You can keep them if you choose, but you will also have to keep all that comes with them. And you will lose all of the things you might gain if you let them go. Really think. You may believe you are giving up something, but you are not. You are just burning away the rot that is keeping you from having a new house, a big new house.

There is nothing to be afraid of. When you add the ingredient of forgiveness to your marriage, it's like you've been flying in the clouds and all of a sudden you're out of the clouds and the sun shines like gold all around you. You will go from being in the doghouse to being your wife's superhero again. You can do anything when she is on your side, when she becomes the cheerleader for your team. What man in his right mind wouldn't want that?

We've told you the reasons why forgiveness is so important to the recipe of an amazing marriage. But what happens if your spouse won't forgive? What happens if your husband or wife doesn't feel like they need to ask for forgiveness? We humbly suggest you practice forgiveness anyway.

Forgiveness does not mean you condone wrong actions toward you. And please do not think forgiving means staying put in an abusive situation. Forgiveness does not mean you give permission to anyone to keep hurting you. It simply means you are letting yourself off the hook from all those negative emotions that have been keeping you bound. Forgiveness means you get a clean heart, a right relationship with God, and hope for a better future.

We can't predict what will happen in your marriage if both partners do not agree to start again from scratch, but we can promise you forgiveness works wonders in your own heart, literally. Scientific studies show negative emotions such as bitterness and unforgiveness create chemical and hormonal imbalances, affecting your heart health.[1] The Mayo Clinic says forgiveness, on the other hand, leads to better heart health, lower blood pressure, a stronger immune system, and fewer symptoms of depression.[2]

"Forgiveness means you get a clean heart, a right relationship with God, and *hope* for a better future."

If you choose to forgive and ask for forgiveness, you will be healthier and ready with the right attitude for God to guide you through, no matter what happens next in your marriage.

Fresh, Quality Flavor: Our No-Fail Recipe

INGREDIENTS:

1 cup of humility
2 willing hearts
2 heaping tablespoons Secret Sauce
1 horizontal connection
Paper and pen
2 out-loud confessions

DIRECTIONS:

Take a full cup of humility and put it before God. Ask God to forgive you and help you forgive your spouse. Pour in two willing hearts who will take paper and pen and each write a list of all the hurts they've caused, all the mistakes they've made, and all the wrongs they've done. Stir in the horizontal connection and have husband and wife confess their lists aloud to each other. Blend in the giving and receiving of forgiveness until smooth.

Fresh, Quality Flavor: Our No-Fail Recipe Card

From the Kitchen of: _____

INGREDIENTS:

_____

_____

_____

_____

_____

_____

_____

DIRECTIONS:

_____

_____

_____

_____

_____

_____

_____

_____

_____

_____

Chocolate Mousse in a Blender

INGREDIENTS:

1 cup semisweet chocolate chips

1 egg at room temperature

1 teaspoon coffee liqueur or vanilla extract

1 cup heavy cream

1/2 cup fresh berries (optional)

Fresh whipped cream (optional)

DIRECTIONS:

Place chocolate chips, egg and coffee liqueur or vanilla in blender and chop.

Heat cream until very hot and small bubbles appear at edge. Carefully pour hot cream into the blender. Blend until chocolate is melted and mixture is smooth.

Pour into dessert dishes or pretty wine or martini glasses. Cover with plastic wrap and refrigerate until it firms up a bit.

Serve with fresh berries and/or whipped cream on top.

Chocolate Mousse in a Blender

NOTE FROM LAINE AND STEVE:

We chose this recipe because by simply blending these ingredients together, the result is sweetly amazing. Each ingredient is vital to produce the right taste, and when you combine it all, just like when you blend the right ingredients in your marriage, you get a great result.

NOTES:

_____

_____

_____

_____

_____

_____

_____

_____

_____

_____

_____

_____

_____

_____

_____

CHAPTER FOUR

All~Natural, Nothing Artificial

Unconditional Love

*"Cooking is like love. It should be
entered into with abandon or not at all."*
Julia Child

*"A successful marriage requires falling in love many times,
always with the same person."*
Mignon McLaughlin

When Steve and I met and fell in love, we never dreamed the day
would come when the idea of divorce would seem like a relief. I
don't think any couple falls in love or gets married thinking they'll
hate each other one day with every bit as much passion as the fiery

love they felt in the beginning of their relationship. Every couple thinks their love is special. Their marriage can overcome anything. Nothing could tear them apart.

Yet more than half of all marriages in the United States end in divorce. The number of couples who live together without the commitment of marriage is at an all-time high. Young people who grew up in broken families bouncing back and forth between mom's house and dad's house express fear of committing to someone for a lifetime in marriage.

If people are still falling in love every day, convinced they'll be together forever, why are so many marriages falling apart? Why are people afraid to get married at all?

We believe a big part of the problem lies with love. Well, not actual love but the artificial love our culture sells us our entire lives.

Think back to the first time you ever tasted a diet soda sweetened with one of the chemical substitutes for sugar. Honestly, do you remember the way you made a face at the terrible aftertaste it left in your mouth? If you're like me, you started drinking them because you thought they'd be better for you than drinking regular soda with all that sugar in it. Diet drinks tasted really bad, but you kept drinking them anyway until you couldn't taste the difference anymore. In fact, if you're a regular diet soda drinker, you've probably gotten so used to the chemical taste that sodas with real sugar now taste awful.

When sugar substitutes first appeared on the market, everyone raved about them. They could help people reduce their sugar consumption. They would help us lose weight and be healthier. Today, scientific study after scientific study reveals how much worse for our bodies the man-made chemicals are than sugar, a natural product from a God-created plant.

Same goes with love. The media's efforts to make romance seem magical and our culture's belief that our life's goal should be the pursuit of individual happiness have replaced God's natural gift of unconditional love with a cheap artificial substitute. We shouldn't be surprised to find statistics proving again and again how far our "improved" version of love falls short of the real thing. We've been fed the fake stuff for so long we have no idea how to recognize, receive, or reciprocate all-natural love.

Think about it. What were you brought up to believe authentic love looks like?

Fairy tales and romance novels teach us that boy meets girl and they fall in love almost instantly. Circumstances temporarily tear them apart, then they magically get back together and ride off into the sunset. "And they lived happily ever after" is the end of the story.

Today's magazines, movies, and other media teach us we have to be unnaturally beautiful, with perfect hair and bodies, before we can even attract the right person for us. Then they teach us to "try out" as many people as we want sexually so we know what we like before we commit.

Our own insecurities teach us unwittingly to use other people's attraction and affection to feel good about ourselves. Our hormones teach us to pursue what our bodies want without considering the consequences. Our bank accounts teach us what's ours is ours and our spouse will take it all unless they sign a prenup.

The broken marriages and family fights we have witnessed teach us to be cynical about whether love can survive or will cost us everything. Our legal system teaches us you can get out of marriage with "no fault" if you fall out of love or feel like you love someone else more. Our well-meaning friends teach us if our spouse hurts us, we deserve better and should walk away. Our culture teaches us if we no longer feel love for our spouse, we should try again with someone new.

Does any of that really sound like true love to you?

It doesn't to us either, but Steve and I didn't recognize how much of the artificial we were preprogrammed to give each other and get in return when we started living our "Once upon a time ..."

We didn't know how much we didn't know about genuine love.

I thought I knew how to give love and receive it. I thought loving well would be as natural as breathing. I'm sure when Steve and I got married I was thinking that everyone says marriage is hard work, but how hard could true love really be? Turns out loving Steve the way he needed to be loved was harder for me than calculus. Loving me the way I needed to be loved was harder for my shy Steve than being the center of attention in a noisy, crowded room.

Why? Because we had never been taught how to recognize, release, or receive real, unconditional, God-designed love. We only had a taste for the fake stuff. If you are struggling in your marriage right now, we bet you were not taught how to recognize, release, or receive the real thing either.

We want to welcome you now to Love Class 101, another vital ingredient in the recipe for reviving your marriage.

If loving and being loved, creating a family, and leaving a legacy that lives on after you're gone are the most valuable things a man can do in life, then why do we grow up taking a lot of classes in reading, writing and arithmetic but no classes at all in commitment, conflict resolution, and caring? There are classes that teach us everything from meteorology to mechanics, from gardening to guitar, but heart-felt love and healthy living are nowhere in the course catalogs.

There is one textbook, however, that contains a full degree program in how to love not just for a lifetime but for all of eternity. It was not written by human culture but by the creator of love, the one who knew you and your spouse and loved you perfectly before you were born (Psalm 139:13-16, Jeremiah 1:5). The Bible exists as an entire love letter to you written by love itself. I John 4:8 (NIV) explains it very simply: "Whoever does not love does not know God, because God is love."

If you want to get an A+ in real love, study God's Word. It has plenty to teach us, and the lessons look nothing like the cheap substitutes we've been taught before. The main theme goes like this: Authentic love is not about you.

That's right. True love can only exist and flourish when it's not about you. Love is not about the way you look, feel, or think. It's not about your plans, dreams, or desires. It's not about what you want, earn, or deserve.

The vital ingredient—real, unconditional love—is added to your life only when you forget all of those things and focus outside yourself. True, fulfilling, thrilling love can naturally sweeten your marriage only when the bitter aftertaste of self-centeredness is rinsed away.

"True, fulfilling, thrilling love can naturally *sweeten* your marriage only when the bitter aftertaste of self-centeredness is rinsed away."

Stop and think about that for a minute. Isn't that a relief? No more worrying about how you look, no more focusing only on how you feel. No more disappointment because you're not getting what you want or anger because your needs aren't being met. No more guilt over temptations or condemning thoughts that you will never be enough. All that disappears the moment you take your eyes off yourself and look straight at your Savior. Then He opens your eyes to truly see the beauty in the spouse He has given you.

I Corinthians 13 says real love is patient and kind. It does not brag and it is not proud. It does not dishonor others or anger easily. It is not selfish or rude. Love keeps no record of wrongs. Love does not delight in evil and rejoices in the truth. Love always (not just when it is convenient or when it feels like it) protects, trusts, hopes and perseveres. Love never fails.

Wow! You know, that description of true love is read again and again at weddings all around the world. Everyone seems to know it is the true standard, but how many try to live it out once the ceremony is over and you get home from the honeymoon?

Biblical love is exactly the kind of love I wanted from my wife even when I hated her. But it looks nothing like the love I was giving her. My version of love included curses, name-calling, and emotional distance. It angered so easily it wasn't even funny, and it kept a mile-long list of her wrongs. The love I gave was rude and acted dishonorably. It was too proud to be vulnerable and truly intimate. My love did not protect, and it certainly didn't trust. My kind of love was ready to walk away, not persevere. It gave up hope in us and our marriage. It definitely failed.

I can hear you thinking, C'mon, Steve. Aren't you being a little hard on yourself? Give yourself and me a break here. I'm only human.

Not so fast. If you are following our recipe for reviving your marriage and you have poured on the Secret Sauce, then you are more than a mere human. The moment you asked your Maker for forgiveness and accepted Jesus' sacrifice for you on the cross, the Bible says the Holy Spirit was given as a gift within you. He lives within you to be your guide, your wisdom, your counselor and comforter. That makes you more than human. In fact, it makes you superhuman. If you ask for it, the Holy Spirit will give you the strength to get rid of all your failed attempts at artificial love and the power to practice true sweet love in their place.

After Steve and I had our **"miracle moment"** of marriage revival when we got down on our knees and asked God and each other for forgiveness, we had to stand back up and start learning how to truly love. We wiped our slates of wrongs clean. Now we had to fill them with the right things. But how could we love the right way if we'd never learned how? God's gold standard of love, all those things listed in 1 Corinthians 13, sounded great but seemed like an impossibly tall order.

1 John 4:8 reminded us if we did not know love and God is love, then we needed to learn new ways of keeping our eyes focused on Jesus and our hearts turned towards each other. From that day forward, our marriage had to become our mission.

In order to start again from scratch and pour real love into our recipe, our Christian counselor asked us to go back in our memories and describe the first time we could remember feeling loved. (More on the importance of solid Christian counseling later.)

We were instructed to share who made us feel loved for the very first time. We described what was happening at the time and what actions made us feel loved by that person. This exercise was pivotal in pointing out where our attempts to love each other fell flat. We believe in order to demonstrate love that will delight your spouse, you must discover the way your spouse first learned to feel loved. Then you can duplicate those actions and draw out your spouse's love.

My memories went like this: I grew up with three older sisters. I had long blonde hair that hung all the way down past my waist, and my sisters loved to practice mothering me. They dressed me up like their little doll. They doted on me. My first memory of feeling loved is when my big sister would brush my hair. The feeling of love for me equaled time and lots of attention.

Steve's first memory of feeling loved was a lot different than mine. He remembered being about eleven years old and riding on a motorcycle behind his dad. His dad kept turning around and looking back to make sure Steve was okay, and that made him feel secure and loved. The feeling of love for Steve equaled someone checking on him to make sure he was doing okay.

Explaining our first feelings of love to each other was eye-opening. I thought Steve had not been trying to love me at all. Steve thought I hadn't been trying to love him at all. After we shared our memories, we realized we actually had been working hard to love each other all along. We were giving love in the ways that made us feel loved. But the ways we felt love were not the same. I was doting on Steve and trying to get him to spend time with me, and he wasn't responding. He was checking on me and asking me how I was doing all the time, and that didn't do it for me.

Discovering this was revelatory. If only we had known it all along. We actually felt pain at all we had lost by not knowing these simple things about love. All Steve needed to feel love was to be checked on, for me to ask if he was okay. How sad is it that in nearly two decades of marriage, my husband was waiting every day for me to ask how he was doing? I don't think I did it even one time.

That exercise on our first memory of love changed everything. Here I was all these years asking Laine how she was doing and she was doting on me and neither of us felt it. We kept piling up layer after layer of resentment in our hearts not only because we weren't getting what we needed, but also because we weren't getting the right reactions to our efforts.

Every time I checked on Laine and asked her how she was doing, I got no good response. I'd keep silently waiting for her to smile at me or thank me for asking, and she didn't even know I was waiting for her to answer. So both of us would keep trying, feel rejected, and then blow up. It was like riding a crazy emotional merry-go-round that went round and round and wouldn't stop. For many long years we never got anywhere and we couldn't get off.

What is your first memory of love? Think back and try very hard to remember. You probably became consciously aware of it when you were somewhere between three and six years old. When did you first feel that you were loved? Close your eyes and go back to that moment. What did it look like? What were you doing? Who were you with? What were the smells and colors? What did that moment feel like? What made it so memorable to you?

You and your spouse can write your answers down if that helps you take yourself back in time. When you're both finished, share your answers with each other. Listen to your spouse carefully. Try to catch every word. Hear their tone of voice. Observe their facial expressions and body language.

Next, take your memories and translate them into triggers. What triggers feelings of love in you now? Do you feel loved when someone does something for you, spends time with you, gives you presents, tells you how awesome you are, touches you? Of course, everyone likes all of these expressions of love, but which one or two make you feel loved the most? Share your conclusions with each other.

Finally, now that you have identified your love triggers, talk out some of the practical ways you can start bringing out feelings of love in each other. Make a list of things your spouse could do or say to make you feel loved. Exchange your lists and start putting them into practice today. Learn to love like your spouse needs to be loved, and you'll both be surprised at how quickly your hearts fill with sweet feelings for each other again. You may feel silly at first or skeptical that such simple acts could really make a difference. Just try it. The natural sweetness of love will fill your hearts and leave no bitter aftertaste!

As you are learning to keep the focus off yourself and to

deposit feelings of love in your spouse, start talking about ways you can make your marriage missional. That may sound a little strange, but all we mean is your marriage should accomplish something bigger than yourselves. What can you do together to help others? How could you minister at your church? Where are you investing your time and talents? What money should you spend to do God's work?

When you bless others instead of living for yourself, you get blessed more than you invest. As a follower of Christ, you do not give in order to get. But when you give, you always receive. That's the paradox of God's economy.

- When you humble yourself, you feel the most fulfilled.

- When you give the most, you receive the most satisfaction.

- When you sacrifice for someone else, your heart gets filled with joy, peace, and contentment.

- When you spend your resources to further the work of God on earth, He gives you more and more to keep spending.

- When you pour out your talents and gifts for the gospel, you get to live with passion and purpose.

- When you give God every bit of your ordinary, He gives you the extraordinary.

- When you give your life to God, He gives you new life with Him for eternity.

When you start working side-by-side on something inspired by God, your love deepens. Your self-centered thinking melts away. All those worries, fears, and frets you had in the past disappear. Confidence in your marriage and in your own God-given abilities grows.

When you are consumed with your problems and pain, the devil has you right where he wants you. The Bible says satan is our enemy. His mission is to steal, kill, and destroy. He just loves to steal our children, kill our marriages, and destroy our families. In fact, I am firmly convinced Christian marriages are his Number One target. Why do I believe that? Because there is so much at stake.

Satan can't get the souls of believers in Jesus Christ. He has already lost us for eternity. All he can do is make us miserable on earth, wasting the little bit of time we have been given to live. That's his goal.

"I am firmly convinced *Christian* marriages are the enemy's No. 1 target. Because there is so much at stake."

When we feel like we are living without love, when we are convinced our spouse can never make us happy, when we walk away from the marriage covenant we made, we allow the enemy to do his dirty work. When the devil successfully shoots down a family, he gets the couple so inwardly focused they can't do any outwardly good. He pulls the kids apart or away from God and their parents, affects future family generations, and takes away the testimony of God's love others could have seen.

Jesus came to give us life, and life more abundantly (John 10:10).When we get our eyes off our problems and onto all the blessings we've been given, we can change the world. Start dreaming big. The sky is not even the limit, only Heaven is. God created the world and everything in it. He owns it all. When you love, follow, and want to serve Him, He calls you His sons and daughters. His heirs. Follow me on that one? God is your dad and He wants to give you all He has. His Word is full of promises to us.

"And God is able to bless you abundantly, so

> that in all things at all times, having all that you
> need, you will abound in every good work."
> —2 Corinthians 9:8 (NIV)

Notice that little word "all." It is repeated three times in that one verse. Evidently, God was trying to emphasize this fact. "All" means all. Every little bit. Not some, in some things, some of the time, so you have some of what you need. Not most things, most of the time, so you have most of what you need. ALL things at ALL times, having ALL that you need. If you jump into the deep end and you can't swim, He promises to provide you with what you need, either a life preserver or the supernatural ability to swim.

Get ready to dive in.

What could you do that is way bigger than your marriage? What have you always wanted to try but knew it would take a miracle to pull off? Our God is in the miracle-making business. Look what he is already working out in your marriage.

"Our God is in the *miracle-making* business."

Listen for His voice. Is He calling you to adopt a bunch of kids into your family, a family on its way to being healthy, healed, and whole? To offer orphans a home where they can grow up with love and fulfill their destiny?

Maybe He wants you to make a difference in a foreign country on the mission field. Maybe you are going to start a business that will be so successful you can financially support some full-time ministries so they can win souls for Christ.

God may call you to teach a Sunday school class, lead a small group in your home, or share your story with other hurting couples. We don't know what your marriage mission will be. But we do know this. When you go where God tells you to go, your life becomes a grand adventure.

One of our life verses that showed Steve and me how much God loves us and how much we need to try to love each other is Ephesians 3:20.

> "Now all glory to God, who is able, through his mighty power at work within us, to accomplish infinitely more than we might ask or think." (NLT)

When we surrender everything in our lives to Jesus, including our marriages, we give God the freedom to work in His power through us. And God can accomplish more through His power in us than we can even *think*. Infinitely more. That gives me goosebumps just thinking about it.

Pour the Secret Sauce of God's salvation and love all over yourself. Give and receive His forgiveness. Practice forgiving each other. Then learn to add a heaping helping of love, love, love. Love God, love each other and you're on your way to cooking up a bountiful buffet of the most delicious dishes this life has to offer. We know firsthand how sweet God's fresh quality, all-natural ingredients taste in our marriage. We can hardly wait until you get a big bite of the feast He's preparing for you.

All-Natural, Nothing Artificial: Our No-Fail Recipe

INGREDIENTS:

1 Corinthians 13 love

2 first memories of feeling loved

2 exchanged lists of ways your spouse can help you feel loved

1 big dream for your marriage mission

DIRECTIONS:

Get out God's cookbook for our lives (the Bible) and turn to 1 Corinthians 13. Read it carefully, adding each ingredient liberally. You cannot add too much of these ingredients.

Pour over each spouse's first memory of feeling loved. Mix in two lists of ways your husband or wife can help you feel their love. Marinate until 1 Corinthians 13 flavors the entire marriage.

Fold in one big dream for your marriage mission. This heart mixture should expand as unconditional love grows and God shows off His power in your lives.

Bake for a lifetime. Share this dish with everyone God puts in your path.

All-Natural, Nothing Artificial: Our No-Fail Recipe Card

From the Kitchen of: _____

INGREDIENTS:

_____

_____

_____

_____

_____

_____

_____

DIRECTIONS:

_____

_____

_____

_____

_____

_____

_____

_____

_____

Best-Ever Pot Roast

INGREDIENTS:

1 (2 to 3 pound) eye of round roast or chuck roast

1 package Hidden Valley Ranch Dressing Mix

1 package McCormick Au Jus Mix

1 stick of butter

5 to 7 pepperoncini peppers

(Optional: Peel 5 to 6 potatoes, wash one bag of baby carrots, and drain two cans of green beans and place around the roast)

DIRECTIONS:

Place roast in slow cooker. Sprinkle top of roast with Ranch Dressing Mix. Then sprinkle Au Jus Mix on top of roast.

Place stick of butter on top of roast. Place pepperoncini peppers around the roast. Then add optional vegetables. Turn slow cooker on low for about 8 hours.

Best-Ever Pot Roast

NOTE FROM LAINE AND STEVE:

We chose this recipe because during all of my (Laine's) growing-up years, my mom prepared a pot roast every Sunday for lunch. As I look back, her loving touch made our family flourish. When you love unconditionally, forgive excessively, and give your life away to others, you will sit down to a legacy-building dinner every time.

NOTES:

_____

_____

_____

_____

_____

_____

_____

_____

_____

_____

_____

_____

CHAPTER FIVE

Herbs and Spices

Kindness, Trust, and Empathy

*"Too often we underestimate the power of a touch, a smile,
a kind word, a listening ear, an honest compliment, or the smallest act
of caring, all of which have the potential to turn a life around."*
Leo Buscaglia

"Few delights can equal the presence of one whom we trust utterly."
George MacDonald

When Steve and I made a commitment to start again from scratch in our marriage, forgiveness came instantly. It really felt like a miracle. Next, we acknowledged the love we had for each other. Then came the harder part. We had to start creating a new recipe for our married life that contained fresher, better ingredients in terms of our everyday words and actions. In order to cook up the feelings of falling in love again, we had to toss in new flavors of communication and behaviors in our relationship. We needed to form new habits.

Galatians 5:22-23 provided a good checklist of "herbs and spices" to flavor our new marital recipe.

> "But the Holy Spirit produces this kind of fruit in our lives: love, joy, peace, patience, kindness, goodness, faithfulness, gentleness, and self-control." (NLT)

Isn't that awesome? It's no wonder we recommend the Bible, right? Just imagine if everyone you meet treated you only with that list of character qualities governing their actions and speech. Life would be pretty sweet, wouldn't it? Now turn that list on yourself. How often are you full of love, joy, peace, patience, kindness, goodness, faithfulness, gentleness, and self-control with your spouse?

I know. Ouch, right?

Believe me, Steve and I can relate. All along I sure wanted him to demonstrate all those qualities to me. I just didn't want to do the same for him. Why? Because he didn't deserve it. He wasn't treating me well.

Actually, yes he did deserve it. He deserves to be treated according to that list simply because he is my husband, and I am called by God to do the right thing no matter what someone else is doing. God directed the apostle Paul to put Galatians 5:22 in the Bible. If I believe the Bible is God's word for my life, a love letter to me to help me and guide me and reassure me that I am loved for eternity, then I can't just gloss over the parts I don't like.

Now you can argue with me all day long, telling me how your spouse doesn't act out any of the Galatians 5:22 list toward you. Why should you act that way first? Why should you treat her nicely when all she does is nag? Why should you have patience with him when he can't even pick up his blankety-blank underwear?

Whatever.

Here's why. Not only does God teach us to in His Word, but also the sooner either spouse starts living life with the fruits of the Spirit thrown into the mix, the faster the flavor of the marriage improves. When someone starts being wonderful all the time, it becomes awfully tough to keep putting the blame on the nice person.

If your husband suddenly became gentle, kind, and patient … all day, every day … I am positive it would be difficult to stay angry, bitter, or filled with hate toward him. Same goes the other way around. If right this minute your wife started acting peaceful, faithful, loving, and joy-filled toward you and stayed that way every day, you'd feel like a pretty big jerk if you kept being mean to her.

It doesn't matter who goes first. The sooner someone does, or you both do, the faster your marriage starts smelling as wonderful as a batch of homemade chocolate chip oatmeal cookies. What's more important to you, being right or being in love and at peace in your own home? At the end of the day, would you rather be able to brag that you got one up on your husband or wife because you worked harder, treated the kids better, or brought home a bigger paycheck? Or would you like to be able to kick back after a long day and relax in the arms of your very best friend before you make sweet love and then drift into peaceful sleep together? If you'd rather "win," you've already lost.

Don't we tell our kids all the time they can't be mean to a brother or sister, just because that sibling was mean first? When you walk in the room and two kids are in a yelling match or are beating each other to a pulp, don't you pull both of them apart? Don't both get the blame? Don't both get in trouble?

On the other hand, if you walk in the room and one child is beating up another child or yelling at the other child and the second child is remaining sweet and calm and trying to bring peace, which child gets in trouble? The one doing the hitting and yelling. Am I right? Marriages in which spouses are constantly attacking each other or one-upping each other have little chance of surviving happily, if at all.

Kindness is one of the first new flavors that can change your marriage completely.

Psychologist John Gottman has studied thousands of couples over the last four decades in order to figure out what makes relationships remain loving. In a famous study he conducted over six years (1986-1992), he discovered that couples were either what he called "masters" or "disasters." Masters were still happy and in love at the end of the six-year period. Disasters had either split up or were extremely unhappy. The primary difference was the amount of *kindness* partners displayed toward each other.

Disasters attacked each other verbally. Every interaction was likely to be tinged with sarcasm or underhanded insults. Physiologically, disaster couples' heart rates were elevated. Gottman said this meant their bodies were in "fight or flight" mode, always ready to attack or defend an attack.

Masters were physiologically calmer, indicating they had more trust in each other. They felt safe with their partner and had greater intimacy. By observing the differences in couples, Gottman says he can now predict with greater than ninety-four percent accuracy which couples will remain happily together and which ones will not. The major determiners are whether each partner brings kindness and generosity to their relationship and whether they display criticism and contempt.

"There's a habit of mind that the masters have," Gottman explained in an interview, "which is this: they are scanning social environment for things they can appreciate and say thank you for. They are building this culture of respect and appreciation very purposefully. Disasters are scanning the social environment for partners' mistakes."[1]

Kindness blossoms in the smallest of words and deeds. If your spouse points something out to you, react positively. For example, if your husband points out a sports car commercial and exclaims over what a cool car it is, agree it is an awesome car. Simple, right? This is how master couples communicate. A spouse in a disaster relationship might ignore the comment altogether, grunt an "uh-huh," or in the worst-case scenario say something like, "Yeah, right. Like you could ever make enough money for us to afford that."

When Steve and I started again from scratch, kindness became a key ingredient to spice up our relationship again.

When Laine and I used to try to communicate before we started again, all of our efforts landed us squarely in the disaster category. If she pushed my buttons I would get angry. Many men use this as their default emotion. I learned that in counseling. Anger feels manly. It covers hurt, jealousy, fear, and just about anything else men feel but don't want to show. The big problem is that anger breeds anger. I called her names. I never laid a hand on her, but my words pounded her heart just like my fists could have pounded her skin. Maybe the words hurt more. She became even better at giving it back. A master at it, actually. We were both always in fight-or-flight mode, ready to go on the offensive or rise to our own defense. And we did plenty of both. It took two of us to destroy our marriage. We got real good at it.

When we agreed to start over, I knew it had to be very different. I thought of our past way of doing marriage like an old falling-down house in the middle of the woods. The foundation was crumbling, the wood was rotten, and everything inside was moldy and rat-infested. And like an old house in the woods, it needed to be burned down to the ground. It would be too costly to do anything else.

We realized, why would we want to bring any of the old crap house with us on our new journey to our new big marital mansion, the house God was going to help us build? We wouldn't. So by confessing, we burned down the old. Then we started moving and following God so He could transform us. We could build the foundation of our new mansion as we grew in our personal relationship with Jesus Christ. Next, we would add the framework of forgiveness, the interiors of love, along with walls of kindness, trust, and empathy. The drywall and plaster of the fruits of the Spirit would complete a new house that could withstand the most severe of storms. Filled with joy, peace, and happiness, we would finally have a true home.

Cooking up a whole new marriage also required rebuilding trust. Wounded hearts become wary, afraid with each conversation or interaction that they are going to get lacerated again. Steve and I had gone after each other for so long we had zero trust in each other. None. I thought he didn't care at all. He thought I was looking for someone else. We betrayed each other and our marriage vows badly.

When we threw the burnt marriage out and gathered the ingredients for a new life, we knew trust would be a biggie. The good advice we received was to lay everything out on the table all at once and, wait for it, leave it there. No rehashing it over and over. No reliving it in our heads or harboring any of it in our hearts. Once it was out and forgiven, it had to be thrown out with the rest of the mess, never to be put back into our new recipe again.

That was hard for me, I'm telling you, not to let my mind wander to the past. At first, it was a constant struggle. Now I don't think about those years at all. I think about today and our future. I allow myself to be more vulnerable with Steve and tell him I love him. I had all these walls I had built, and I had to tear them down. Now I want to show him I care. I want to know whether or not he is okay.

Believe me, the only way to rebuild trust with your spouse is to refuse to go back in your thoughts and words to the bad times.

When you want to go back to those hurt places like sticking your tongue in a sore tooth, you can literally say, "Get thee behind me, satan." With God in your life, you have the power to tell the devil to get lost. Just kick his ugly butt out the door of your home. Do not listen to his voice telling you lies in your own head. Stand up. Speak out loud. Grab your Bible. Pray with your spouse. Call a friend. Do whatever it takes not to listen to lies that say you will never be free of your past.

You both got a clean slate, a "Get out of jail free" card, when you asked for and received forgiveness. Now you have to walk it out every day by beginning to trust each other again. We know it's hard. It might even still seem impossible at this point. But we know you can do it, because we did. We're just ordinary people, a regular couple, nothing special except that we made up our minds to turn our *Titanic* around before the iceberg could sink her. You can too.

Trusting Laine again wasn't easy, but I knew we couldn't have a new marriage without it. Besides, I had committed what I believe is the ultimate sin in marriage: list-keeping. I kept list after list in my head and in my heart of everything Laine had ever done wrong. Everything she had ever done against me. Everything she had ever said against me. Everything she had not done for me. With that kind of attitude, one where I was constantly thinking about everything bad, how could she trust me either?

I wasn't taking care of her. I was not protecting her heart. I was not even interested in her heart. I was only focused on mine.

In order to rebuild trust between me and my wife, I had to throw out all my lists. That meant I had to start taking my thoughts captive. It takes a lot of practice, but you can get really good at it.

> *"We demolish arguments and every pretension that sets itself up against the knowledge of God, and we take captive every thought to make it obedient to Christ."*—2 Corinthians 10:5 *(NIV)*

Okay, Steve, what exactly do you mean? *I mean when any ugly thought comes into your mind, stop it right there. Don't expand it. Don't keep thinking about it. Don't give it room to grow or stick around. Kick it right back out. Tell it to go. Turn your mind to something wonderful about your wife every time a negative thought comes in.*

I make it my daily habit to take my thoughts captive. If a thought comes in that won't help my relationship with my wife, that's okay. They do come in. But I try to get rid of it in about two seconds. A lot of times, I re-read the book of James. It is a really practical book with a lot of great life advice. It helps center me.

Trust couldn't come in until I started talking to my wife again too. I had to open up and share my day with her, tell her about my work. And it was okay because when we started again, she was really interested. She cared and it showed. That made me want to tell her more. I could see respect in her eyes again. And love. I knew if I let down my guard with her, I would be safe. She was designed to be a safe place for me all along. Now I knew she was.

One of the best ways to build trust with each other again is by exposing all the lies, all the half-truths, all the hidden things. This takes place when you ask each other and God for forgiveness. If all of it did not come out back in Chapters Two and Three, it's time to back up and repeat the process. Unpack the rest now. Especially if it is ugly. If you are hiding credit card bills or struggling with pornography, out with it all. Your marriage cannot become delicious when you are secretly adding spoiled ingredients to the mix.

You cannot have a great-tasting recipe for marriage unless the truth, the whole truth, and nothing but the truth is on the table. Then you forgive, throw the garbage out, and start again with a goal of complete honesty from that moment forward. Do not cry secret tears from your husband. Do not fume behind your wife's back. Do not go to a friend or coworker and confide all the things your spouse is doing wrong. Take your issues to each other with love, remembering to create an atmosphere filled with all those "fruits" (love, joy, peace, patience, kindness, gentleness, etc.), especially when you have to confront difficult subjects. It is also very important for both of you to talk about what bugs you without making the other spouse defensive. Start your sentences with "I feel" instead of pointing a finger by starting with "You."

> "You cannot have a great-tasting recipe for marriage unless the *truth*, the whole truth, and nothing but the truth is on the table."

Another way our trust broke down was I did not know how to tell Steve what I needed from him for a long time. I expected him to just know. Ladies, if you have not figured it out by now, men are not ever going to be mind readers. No, your husband really did not know you wanted that chocolate bar when he asked but you were afraid he would think you were being a pig so you said no! If you want the candy bar, admit it. Or at least admit you are not having it because you are worried about what he would think. Positive honesty works a lot better than keeping him in the hot seat guessing. Most men base their responses on the exact words you speak. They are not designed to be good at reading between the lines.

Men, you need to say more than "okay" when we ask how your

day was and say more than "nothing" when we ask what you are thinking about. We wives long to know you. We want to hear about your bad days and your good ones. We almost always try to read between the lines, not relying on what your words said. We listen for tone. We react to body language. We can sense when there is more to the story. Please share it with us.

In your new recipe for marriage, making plans and setting goals are great ways to begin rebuilding trust. It gives you something to talk about and work toward together. It takes the focus off of any remaining problems and gives you something new to strive for side-by-side.

Taking a "break," a "pause," or a "time-out" from your issues also builds trust. Create a buzz word you will both remember and use it whenever either of you starts to get angry. Take that time to do something fun together without talking about your problems until you are both calm and feel safe to share again. Take a walk, go out to eat, work in the garden, ask your kids to put on a show, or get on the exercise equipment together. Remember what you like about each other and how valuable your marriage is before tackling the tough talk again.

Rebuilding trust, like practicing kindness, may take some time before it's a habit that comes naturally. That's normal. It's completely okay. Remember, this is a recipe for a no-fail marriage. Recipes take time to get the new ingredients, assemble them in the right amounts, mix them all together and cook them into an awesome dish.

Empathy is a word you probably don't think about much, if at all. I know I didn't. But it's a little word that packs a powerful punch. Without it, any relationship is almost guaranteed to fail. Empathy is close to sympathy, but to me there is a big difference.

When I feel sympathy for someone, I feel compassion for them. I feel sorry for what they are going through. Sympathy is an important quality too. But empathy is crucial. Empathy means I try to feel what another person is feeling. I want to identify with or share vicariously their feelings, thoughts and attitudes. Basically, it's that old expression about walking a mile in someone else's shoes. When a partner goes from wanting the best for you to seeing the negative in you, that's a lack of empathy. We don't want to walk in the other guy's shoes. We just get resentful that he or she is stepping on our toes. Trust, kindness, and empathy must all blend into our new recipe for marriage.

Why is empathy crucial? Because empathy takes the focus off yourself and puts it where it belongs—on God and your spouse. Empathy gives you the ability to think about what God is feeling toward you and your marriage, what His attitude would be in any situation. It reminds you that your wife's shoes are not always comfortable. Empathy helps you understand how she feels and thinks when you say and do things. It is a great barometer for how sweet you are making your marriage for her.

Of course, empathy is best when it is extended both ways. You need empathy from your wife like you need air to breathe. Now don't get me wrong. Empathy from your wife does not make you weak at all. It just means your wife is thinking about how you would feel before she acts or speaks. Wouldn't that be great?

Dr. Willard F. Harley, Jr. explains well what happens in marriage when there is a lack of empathy:

> *"Lack of empathy helps make thoughtlessness possible. Since we don't feel what others feel, we tend to minimize the negative effects we have on others, and consider our thoughtlessness to be benign. An angry outburst is regarded by some as a creative expression. Disrespect is viewed as*

helping the other spouse gain proper perspective. And a demand is nothing more than encouraging a spouse to do what he or she should have done all along. None of these is seen as one spouse gaining at the other's expense, because the spouse who is inflicting the pain does not feel the pain ... I call all the ways that spouses are inconsiderate of each other's feelings Love Busters because that is what they do—they destroy the love that a husband and wife have for each other."[2]

I want to be a love maker, not a love buster. Don't you?

Before we started creating our no-fail recipe and reviving our marriage, I really did not have any empathy for Steve at all. All I could think about was what he was not doing for me. He was not making enough money so we could not live in the kind of house I thought we should be living in. I could not go to the mall and buy that new bag when I wanted to. He kept drilling those ridiculous dry holes when maybe he should go out and get a real job with a real paycheck. Why couldn't he see how tired I was? Why couldn't he see that I wanted him to brush my hair like my sisters did or make me feel special?

I wasn't interested in how Steve was feeling, because my own negative feelings were overwhelming me and pushing out anything else. Lack of empathy was a huge problem for me. One I didn't even stop to think twice about for a long time. When I got sick of myself and realized all my pouting, nagging, ignoring, and being angry weren't getting any positive attention from Steve, I realized I'd never be able to change him. The only person I could change was myself. That's when empathy could finally come in.

You can't be empathetic when you can only see and hear yourself. You have to get out of the way, Girlfriend, and let God work on your husband while you also let God work on you. And the other way around. Husband, please beg God to give you new eyes, new ears, new thoughts, and a new heart for your wife. Ask Him to give you the gift of reading between her lines, of paying attention to her tone and body language.

Being empathetic means you do not get defensive or angry if your spouse walks in with a frustrated or accusing tone. Instead, empathy demands you think first about why your spouse is speaking that way. Empathy helps you quickly assess whether your spouse is upset with you or just having a bad day and accidentally taking it out on you. Empathy keeps you on each other's side at all times. Empathy wants to get to the heart of the matter so your spouse can feel better. Empathy allows you then to express how your spouse's tone or words made you feel in a way that your spouse can hear without getting defensive or upset again. Empathy is an amazing ingredient for a healthy marriage recipe.

> **"Empathy keeps you on each other's side at *all* times."**

Take those steps toward being vulnerable with each other and with God, pour in liberal amounts of kindness, and allow your hearts to open up again and feel empathy for each other. With the herbs and spices of kindness, trust, and empathy, your new marriage will soon be simmering nicely. When something on the stove is simmering when you walk in from a long day, the whole house smells good. Your stomach rumbles for a taste of that goodness. Your mouth waters for that meal.

Is your mouth watering yet?

Herbs and Spices: Kindness, Trust, and Empathy Our No-Fail Recipe

INGREDIENTS:

1 forgiven and loved husband

1 forgiven and loved wife

Liberal amounts of the herbs and spices Kindness, Trust, and Empathy, to taste

DIRECTIONS:

Take one forgiven, loved husband and one forgiven, loved wife and place in a freshly started marriage. Have each spouse add liberal amounts of kindness, trust, and empathy to the marriage. Keep folding these ingredients into the marriage to taste.

Note: It may take a lot of these herbs and spices before you begin to taste the difference. There is no limit on the amount of Kindness, Trust, and Empathy that can be used. These ingredients can never hurt the new recipe, only enhance it.

Herbs and Spices:
Our No-Fail Recipe Card

From the Kitchen of: _____

INGREDIENTS:

_____
_____
_____
_____
_____
_____
_____

DIRECTIONS:

_____
_____
_____
_____
_____
_____
_____
_____
_____

Fried Chicken

INGREDIENTS

2 (3-pound) frying chickens, cut up, washed and patted dry

2 tablespoons chopped garlic (about 8 large cloves)

4 cups buttermilk or plain yogurt, stirred until smooth

3 cups unbleached all-purpose flour

Lard or peanut oil, for frying

HERB AND SPICE MIX:

1/2 teaspoon ground cayenne pepper

1 teaspoon freshly ground cumin

1/2 teaspoon ground mace

1 teaspoon freshly grated nutmeg

1 teaspoon paprika

1 teaspoon freshly milled black pepper

1 teaspoon ground ginger

2 teaspoons crumbled dried basil

2 teaspoons ground bay leaves

2 teaspoons crumbled dried oregano

2 teaspoons crumbled dried sage

2 teaspoons crumbled dried thyme

1 teaspoon salt

DIRECTIONS:

Place chicken in a large glass or stainless steel bowl. Stir garlic into buttermilk or yogurt. Pour over chicken. Refrigerate 30 to 60 minutes.

Meanwhile, combine Herb and Spice Mix ingredients in a bowl and stir until evenly mixed. Place flour and Herb and Spice Mix in a paper bag or large zipper bag. Close bag and shake until the seasoning is well-distributed.

To serve hot, preheat the oven to 150 degrees. Fit a wire cooling rack on a cookie sheet and set aside. Fill a Dutch oven or deep-fat fryer with enough lard or oil to come halfway up the sides. On the stove over medium-high heat, bring the fat to 375 degrees (hot but not smoking).

Beginning with the dark meat, lift chicken pieces out of the marinade one at a time, allowing the excess to flow back into the bowl, and drop them into the bag with the seasoned flour. Close the bag and shake until chicken is well coated. Shake off the excess flour, and slip enough pieces into the fat to fill the pan or fryer without crowding it. Deep-fry until the outside is a rich brown and the chicken is tender, maintaining the temperature at 365 degrees about 15 to 20 minutes, turning the chicken once, if necessary.

Remove the pieces as they are done, drain well, and place on the wire rack set in a cookie sheet. If you plan to serve it hot, keep the finished chicken in warm oven while you fry the second batch.

NOTE FROM LAINE AND STEVE:

We picked this recipe because it's a lot of work. It takes a bunch of herbs and spices, and you have to work hard to get it right. However, just like marriage restoration, when it's done right it's more than worth it.

Directions

*"From morning till night, sounds drift
from the kitchen, most of them familiar and
comforting....On days when warmth is the
most important need of the human heart, the
kitchen is the place you can find it; it dries
the wet sock, it cools the hot little brain."*
E. B. White

Mix the Right Measures

Setting Priorities Straight

"Cooking is like painting or writing a song. Just as there are only so many notes or colors, there are only so many flavors — it's how you combine them that sets you apart."
Wolfgang Puck

"Decide what you want, decide what you are willing to exchange for it. Establish your priorities and go to work."
H. L. Hunt

When Steve and I started talking about what needed to be different in our marriage for it to become brand new, we agreed right away we needed a new set of directions to follow. We had added some of the wrong ingredients to our marital recipe, and not nearly enough of some of the right ones. Once we listed the ingredients that needed to be part of our marriage, we had to figure out how to measure the right amounts of each one.

When you are standing in the kitchen assembling all the items needed to make a wonderful meal, you can't throw the same amounts of everything into your mixing bowl, pour it all in the pan to cook, and expect it to turn out tasty. You have to choose your ingredients carefully, measure them correctly, and add them in the right order.

When we started reviving our marriage, we knew we only had a certain amount of some ingredients. A limited number of twenty-four hours in a day. A limited amount of money to spend.

Other ingredients like love and the "herbs and spices" of joy, peace, patience, trust, and kindness we could add to taste. You never have to run out of ingredients like those if you take care to keep them in abundant supply. A little more joy, peace, and kindness can be added liberally to your mixture any time to keep your marriage fresh.

But back to the limited ingredients. Time and money, the finite elements that will remain in limited supply until we get to Heaven, have to be mixed in the right measures to get the best marriage. There is just no way to work around this. A marriage with little time invested becomes a marriage that flops. A marriage with time invested in the wrong things gets burnt to a crisp. A marriage that bakes just right for a lifetime, giving off a delicious smell and tasting even better, requires time to cook at just the right temperature.

The most important basic ingredient is time. Time becomes the base. Then you add all those herbs and spices you need for your marriage. Your relationship with God and your spouse must become the most important thing in your life. More important than work. More important than the kids. You need to be marriage-focused until making your marriage a priority becomes a habit.

What does it take to be marriage-focused with your time? It may mean quitting individual hobbies or sports like scrapbooking with the girls or basketball after work with the guys for a while. It may mean taking a leave of absence from civic obligations, volunteer commitments, clubs, or church ministries. It may mean cutting back on kid activities and extracurriculars. We can't tell you what it will look like in your marriage. All we can tell you is that your relationship as a couple has to become Number One in your time and attention. Burnt-up marriages cannot be repaired and revived without time. It just won't happen. Only God should get more attention than your marriage and family.

> **"You need to be marriage-focused until making your marriage a *priority* becomes a habit."**

Besides, if you have just spent months, years, or decades emotionally draining each other or living with depression and dysfunction, it takes time to reset your emotional compasses. You are healing from post traumatic marital stress syndrome. You need rest. You need a healthy diet. You need downtime and fun time. You need time to learn to talk to each other, time to form new communication habits, time to be vulnerable and intimate, even time to spice up your sex life.

There is nothing you can substitute for time. Nothing should override your new commitment to your marriage. Take your energy and life and pour it back into your relationship with one another. Remember, you are back to the beginning. It's as if you just met and started dating. By investing time in your marriage, you will soon want to spend more time with your spouse. You will look forward to it. The faster you start prioritizing, setting goals, and learning to play and plan together, the more exciting your marriage will become.

At the lowest point in our marriage, I certainly did not dream of spending time with my wife. I dreamed about getting divorced, moving to Houston, buying me a nice car and finding some new girls who would be happy with me and treat me better.

But think about it really. Like your daydreams of a perfect vacation, it's never perfect once you get there because you have filled your imagination with all the fun you will have, all the good things you'll experience, without factoring in any of the bad things that will inevitably come up. Like bad food, a sunburn or misplaced reservations. The perfect vacation is never perfect. Your vision is an illusion. My vision of a new life was too. Still, for a long time I figured my daydreams were better than the nightmare I had at home. I was wrong.

When I agreed to forgive Laine and start our marriage over, I won the first big battle. It was the battle in my own mind of choosing good over choosing evil. Keeping my marriage together, protecting my family, was good. Leaving it was evil.

However, if I was going to stay and start again from scratch, I knew I had to do it all the way. We would wind up right back in the middle of our great big mess if we changed nothing in our marital recipe. If we did nothing more than ask for forgiveness and went back to our fifty- or sixty-hour work weeks and our exhaustion, we would never make it.

In the first few minutes after we decided to try again, prayed together, and exchanged forgiveness, our marriage was fixed. All of it. We just didn't know how to live together like it was fixed yet. That's where time becomes absolutely critical.

We began going to a Christian counselor (one of the new uten-

sils we added to our kitchen tools. More on that in Chapter Seven.), and one of the first things the counselor told us to do was start dating again.

Our first date was going out to dinner and a movie. We got dressed up for each other, something we had not done in a long time. It was awkward at first in the car and when we got to the restaurant, but soon we started talking about anything and everything, just like we had in the beginning. We held hands. That felt like a miracle right there. We wanted to be connected. We smiled and laughed. When she looked at me on that first date, didn't yell at me about the kids, seemed happy to be with me, I looked in her eyes and it was like the devil wasn't looking at me anymore.

Dating again feels wonderful. When you leave the struggles behind and don't bring them to the table with you and your date, talk about a breath of fresh air. You ought to seriously treat it as if this is a totally new person you are dating. That helps you recognize whenever old habits of accusing or blaming try to creep in. It's hard to make it feel like a date if you are griping at each other or complaining.

In order to go to counseling and to date my wife, I had to reset my priorities. I had to be determined nothing was going to come between me and my marriage. If you are starting again from scratch with your wife or your husband, both of you have to become downright bullheaded about this. God and your marriage come first. Period. End—no, the beginning—of your new story. Starting now and for the rest of your lives.

When you put your marriage first, you can get a lot more work done in a lot less time because your attitude and outlook become positive. Your focus and productivity increase. When I got my priorities straight, I realized I could work again. I didn't even know how ineffective I had become. I was putting in the long hours and nothing was coming through, probably because of all the negative, all the baggage, all the problems. With God, lengthy hard things *became short easy things.*

After we started dating, Laine became my cheerleader. Now she appreciated when I went to work instead of getting angry with me for not spending time with her because I had to work. Now she was grateful I was investing time not only in her, but also in my work to try to keep us from poverty. I became her hero again. Personally, I think that is all any guy wants. To become his wife's hero.

Once again, my wife, my sons, and my daughter were all proud of my efforts. When you feel like the king of your house, you are the king of everything again. That, my friend, changes everything.

I never dreamed Steve could love me like I thought he should. Call me beautiful? No way. Leave work a little early to take me on a date? Are you kidding me? At the darkest hour in our marriage I had no hopes of Steve ever being able to love me as a lover and a friend. I didn't think he would ever show me the attention another man could. He would never say the sweet nothings, like how beautiful or sexy I was. He would never tell me what an incredible businesswoman I was. No, I could only hear his negative words in my head. I was convinced he didn't even want to be around me.

Once Steve and I made up our minds to start again from scratch, confessed and gave our lives to God, and forgave one another, we started a great adventure. It has become the trip of a lifetime. It was the journey to discovering how to love each other so that we each felt it. One step at a time, we learned how to trust again and care about each other again. I started allowing my heart to believe Steve was my knight in shining armor, the hero I longed for to rescue me. My heart was willing to take a chance on falling in love with my own husband again. I dared to risk the pain of getting stabbed in the heart again because I knew we both deserved a chance to start again from scratch with the one we first fell in love with when we said "I do."

I wondered if our "first date" after seventeen years of marriage could be romantic and fun. It was! We laughed so hard we cried. We didn't focus on the kids or negative things. We acted as if we were really on a first date. You don't bring baggage on your first date with someone new. We kept it light. We acted as if we didn't know the details of our own lives. In some ways, we had been so far apart we didn't. We asked all kinds of questions. Our very first date after being married for seventeen years was remarkable.

As we continued dating again, it kept getting better. After years of not even wanting to be in the same room, it was exciting to look at my husband with my eyes finally opened to his good qualities instead of only the bad. It was fun to dress up and look the best I could compared to dressing up to go out among strangers.

> "As we continued *dating* again, it kept getting better."

I loved seeing Steve smile again. He was beaming just because we were together. I couldn't remember the last time I had seen such happiness in his face. Or mine either, for that matter.

A dash of date nights (not too many because we still didn't have any money), a dollop of sweet notes by the coffee pot, and a splash of some occasional flowers kept making our recipe better and better. Before hardly any time passed, Steve and I were falling back in love. We were making our marriage matter. We were demonstrating our love through prioritizing our marriage at the top of our to-do list. We mixed in small gestures physically and gave each other the most valuable gift we could give, time with our hearts one hundred percent in it.

Steve would make my day just by leaving a special note by the coffee pot on the mornings he would leave early. Just a note to wish me a good day. The words "I love you" brought me to tears every time. Just a few small words on a sticky note made my heart melt for my own husband. I began to forget all the things Steve did not do for me and see all the little ways he was trying. I began to long for my husband. We were creating what you see in the movies right there in our own home. These small notes were huge deposits into my love bank, and my love for him began to overflow. No more disrespect. No more secret longings for another prince charming. No more dreams of a better man. Not when I was beginning to have the man I had always wanted.

> "Just a few small words on a sticky note made my heart *melt* for my own husband."

For any marriage that needs to start again, the most basic ingredient for success is time. Time was all we had, the most valuable thing we owned. Even money can't buy time. We all have an expiration date on our lives and in the relationships we create. Steve and I made a commitment, a pact, that we were going to put our marriage before anything.

My schedule required a total makeover in the reviving of our marriage. No more going out for me at night. No more business meetings that would take priority over our counseling. Not one thing would take precedence over my time with Steve.

The rewards came quickly. Both of us knew we had chosen to be together. We could have made choices to be somewhere else. Each time we went out together or spent time at home together, we made deposits in what you could call "love accounts." Immediately, love began to grow again. The desire to be together grew. We were becoming friends, companions, and lovers instead of enemies on opposing teams. Our good times transformed us into what we had always wanted to be in the first place, a loving couple who could make it happily to the end.

What's holding you back from giving your most valuable commodity, time, to your marriage? What needs to be taken out of your calendar so you can pencil in those date nights? What needs to be done to make connecting with your spouse the priority? You can't wait for time to open up. It won't. You can't wait until you get through this season. The next season comes right on its heels. You can't wait until you have made a little more money. What good will the money be if your family falls apart?

Start today. Start right now. Plan your first date night for this week. Take turns planning them and try to outdo each other. Be creative. Have fun. You can do this.

Ready? Set? Go!

Mix the Right Measures: Our No-Fail Recipe

INGREDIENTS

1 overworked, overcommitted, exhausted husband

1 overworked, overcommitted, exhausted wife

1 or 2 calendars (paper, cell phones, laptops or whatever system works to keep you both on schedule)

2 cups determination to reset your priorities

1 date night per week

As many hours per week spent with each other as needed to sweeten your recipe

Add babysitters as needed

DIRECTIONS:

Take the overworked, overcommitted, exhausted husband and wife and have them sit down together with their calendars. Plan time for talking daily, just to connect. Pencil in one date night each week. Take turns choosing the activities and lining up the logistics (babysitter, reservations, budget, etc.).

Take the 2 cups of determination and puree the whole mix, blending the determination thoroughly into the spouses. Spend time together. Have fun together. Get to know each other again. Repeat until you have acquired such a taste for this recipe that you crave it all the time.

Mix the Right Measures: Our No-Fail Recipe Card

From the Kitchen of: _____

INGREDIENTS:

_____
_____
_____
_____
_____
_____
_____

DIRECTIONS:

_____
_____
_____
_____
_____
_____
_____
_____
_____

Veal Picatta

INGREDIENTS

1/2 cup all-purpose flour, mixed with 1 1/2 teaspoons salt and
 1/2 teaspoon freshly ground black pepper

4 veal scallops, about 3/4 pound, pounded to 1/8-inch thick

1 1/2 tablespoons vegetable oil

5 tablespoons butter, divided

1 cup dry white wine

1/2 cup chicken stock

1 garlic clove, chopped

Juice of 1 lemon (about 2 tablespoons), or more to taste

2 tablespoons capers, drained

1/2 teaspoon salt

1 tablespoon chopped parsley leaves, optional

DIRECTIONS:

Dredge (coat) veal in flour mixture. Heat oil in a large skillet over medium-high heat until very hot. Add 1 1/2 tablespoons butter and cook veal until golden, 1 minute per side. Transfer to plate.

Deglaze pan with wine by bringing to a boil and scraping browned bits from the pan. When wine has reduced by half, add stock, garlic, lemon juice and capers. Cook 5 minutes, or until sauce has thickened slightly. Whisk in salt, remaining 3 1/2 tablespoons butter and parsley. Return veal to pan, and heat through. Serve immediately.

Veal Picatta

NOTE FROM LAINE AND STEVE:

We gave you this recipe because it looks difficult and time-consuming, but when you line everything up, it can be simple and fast. Line up time for your relationship, and positive results will come faster than you think.

NOTES:

_____

_____

_____

_____

_____

_____

_____

_____

_____

_____

_____

_____

_____

_____

_____

CHAPTER SEVEN

Use the Right Utensils

Putting Tools in Your Toolbox

*"I'm going to use all my tools, my God-given ability,
and make the best life I can with it."*
LeBron James

*"The kitchen is a country in which there are always discoveries
to be made."*
Grimod de la Reynière

Okay, guys, Steve here. I get to start this chapter because it's all about the right utensils. Imagine you just got a new red toolbox, Stanley or whatever. What tools have you been using for marriage, for your life? You probably need some new ones. The ones you have are worn out, and they were probably the wrong tools to begin with or else you would have already fixed everything. You just need to get the tools that will make the job easy and right. Then you can begin fixing your marriage until it starts to look and smell like something you can be proud of.

One of the most important full-package sets of tools, an essential one really, is great counseling. Great Christian counseling. Somehow, the devil has convinced most men this is not a good thing. First, let me tell you, it was the easiest thing I did and the best money I spent. I said things a hundred times at home and my wife wouldn't listen or argued about it. Then the counselor said the same thing, and I could just smile.

Hey, if you can't fix your toilet, you don't just live with that thing running all the time or spewing out sewage all over your bathroom floor indefinitely. You pay a plumber to get to your house quickly and repair it, right? If you don't know how to get your car running, you get a trained mechanic. If your cell phone screen is smashed to smithereens, you take it in to the professionals for new glass. So why would it be any different for a broken marriage? Going to counseling simply means you a choose to pay a professional to get it fixed right.

Qualified, certified, educated counselors spend years absorbing all kinds of tricks and techniques to make relationships improve. They took all the college courses and classes on behaviors and personalities and communication styles so you don't have to. When you pay for an hour of their time, you get the condensed notes you need to pass the tests instead of having to read every word of the textbooks. It is a shortcut. Counselors are trained to see the root of the problems and know how to offer helpful suggestions for fixing them. People only have about seven or eight major common issues. All of us deal with a few of them. Hiding them is a trick of the devil. If they are hidden, then they grow. Brought to light, they are easy to fix.

When you get a new car, you want to take care of it, detail it, keep it running well. You wouldn't get a beautiful new car and then not service it, not change the oil. If you did, it would burn up. Well, did you pay special attention to detail and change the oil in your marriage? Did it burn up? Counseling is a utensil that keeps your marriage pot from boiling over all the time. It's like those wooden spoons you use when the foam starts rising on a bubbling pot of spaghetti noodles or rice. You need to take that utensil and stir vigorously to keep the hot concoction cooking but not overflowing everywhere, burning everything it touches. Counseling by a professional may be the easiest utensil to buy and the best money you spend. After all, if you turn your marriage around, the dividends will last a lifetime.

Both of you should go to the same counselor so the counselor can work on bringing you together, helping you find new connection and common ground. Laine started going to counseling first. She decided she needed to talk to somebody because we sure couldn't talk to each other. My smart response was, "Sure, you pick out the counselor, so you get the one you want." I didn't want that to be an issue or excuse. If the counselor she picked was awful or against me, I'd deal with that later.

The first three months Laine's counselor wanted to see her alone, and I tried not to think about it much. Time would tell what Laine revealed and what the counselor said. Imagine how surprised I was when Laine came home one evening, found me in the garage at the drafting table, and planted a big kiss right on my lips. Now this was a woman who hadn't gone out of her way to touch me in months, except when she pierced me with those daggers that shot out of her eyes all the time at me. I'm telling you I wondered if she had finally lost it when she marched up, pasted her lips on mine, then said, "There. My counselor told me to do that."

Okay, now I had my answer. This counselor was pro-marriage. Good. God took care of that one for me. We added other utensils too, like a weekend Christian retreat experience called Cursillo that was life-changing. You can read good books, attend marriage courses at a local church or even at some community colleges. Invest time and even money in some great utensils. Otherwise, it's like working on a sixty-thousand-dollar vehicle with a five-dollar cheap-o wrench set. Your marriage is worth more than that.

Once we got these new utensils to use in our recipe for marriage, life really started looking up. With my wife and her Christian counselor on my side, how could I lose? The new tools worked, and everything kept turning around.

I didn't know it at the time, but that kiss my counselor told me to give Steve was the first pinch of spice that would go into our yet-to-come miracle marriage recipe. What happened was that in one of my counseling sessions, I shared how hurt I was when I had come home from a recent business trip. Steve had not even bothered to kiss me hello when he picked me up from the airport. I told her all about how he did not want me and did not make an effort to love on me.

Sure, he showed up and threw my suitcase in the car. But where was the love? I fumed silently all the way home. I felt so unloved. I had been gone and he did not even welcome me back. I was sure he had not missed me. I thought he probably wished I would have just stayed gone forever.

I told my counselor this story because I just knew she would understand exactly how I felt. She would see clearly what a cold, heartless man I had for a husband.

Only she didn't. She shocked me by asking one simple question.

"Laine, why didn't you just kiss him?"

Instead of watching and waiting for Steve to get it wrong, she put me on the spot and asked why I didn't do what I thought would have been right. Maybe Steve didn't know I wanted to be kissed. We certainly were not on very good terms at that point. We hardly touched at all anymore, except for in bed. No matter how angry and bitter we were, we maintained a sex life. Just not much affection outside of our bed.

I stewed over her words all the way home that day. If I wanted to be greeted with a kiss, why didn't I take the initiative? Why didn't I ask for one or lean toward my husband so he would get the hint? Expecting him to read my mind and then mentally crucifying him when he didn't get it right was cruel to both of us. He suffered from my anger without even knowing what he had done wrong. I suffered from hurt and rejection that could have been all in my head.

So when I got home that day, I marched out where Steve was working in the garage and gave him a kiss. The look on his face was priceless. And kissing was nice. I was still mad at him for so many things, but that one small gesture created a little crack in the surface of our ice-cold relationship.

> ## "If I wanted to be greeted with a *kiss*, why didn't I take the initiative?"

The reason I started counseling was because I was tired of the woman I had become. When I looked in the mirror every day, I no longer recognized myself. I was living totally opposite from the way I knew I should be. I looked to myself like Humpty Dumpty who had fallen off the wall. I was a woman in a million pieces. Nothing in my marriage had turned out the way it was supposed to. Misery dogged my steps all the time. I knew I needed something more than I could figure out by myself or clearly I would have changed things for the better a long time ago.

I found a Christian counselor who would see patients on a sliding scale based on their income. Since we had little income, the fee was affordable. I went to the counselor weekly. The first thing I learned was I could only work on me. I could share my feelings about Steve, but I could only change myself. However, if I improved myself, I would feel better and be in a better, healthier place to start over no matter what happened with my marriage. With or without Steve, I could get some new utensils to use in the recipe for a changed life.

Once I understood the counselor was not taking Laine's side and helping her plot against me, I started watching Laine more closely. I began to see changes I liked. She did not seem as angry all the time anymore. Her face looked more at ease. A gradual shift was taking place in my wife and it was fascinating to watch.

When Laine put me on the spot and asked me to start again from scratch, I realigned my schedule to begin counseling too. We needed a professional to help us throw out what we had burnt to a crisp and concoct something fresh and new. We took the process seriously. As hard as we had thrown ourselves into work and one-upping each other before, now we poured all that determination into creating something better in our marriage.

I went to counseling on Mondays, Laine went on Wednesdays, and we had a session together on Fridays. No exceptions. We were so dedicated we put the fees on our credit card when we couldn't afford to pay outright. Today I can say it's the best money we ever spent.

One of the greatest things I got out of counseling was the importance of being completely honest. My counselor made it clear it would be painful, terrifying, and incredibly difficult to lay all my ugliness in front of my husband. I would feel guilt, shame, and terror at the potential outcome. But it's like ripping a bandage off. You need to do it all at once and get it over with. You can't leave a corner of it hanging indefinitely from your skin. Flesh wounds need to be exposed to air and light so they can heal.

Heart wounds do too.

It's too easy for us to justify all the reasons why we allow bad choices and behaviors to damage our lives and our marriages. Then the damage becomes even more severe because of guilt and fear of what revelation will bring. It builds and builds until it has to either boil over or be taken off the heat.

So I had to be totally upfront and open with Steve. If I had left out any part of the truth, even one small detail, I would always wonder if the forgiveness and transformation was real. If it would have occurred at all if I had said that one last tidbit. If anything remained hidden, I would have remained haunted by it. I also would have remained in fear it would be discovered. Without knowing that everything has been revealed and forgiven, you can't create total trust.

While Laine started counseling, I had also been doing some soul searching. For years since the fire that almost destroyed my career, I had talked to God more. I had been seeking answers. I began to read and re-read the book of James. I also noticed that "truth" was a word in the New Testament that kept being repeated again and again. I decided it must be a pretty important word to be used so many times.

Over and over, the Bible talks about living in the truth. You can't live in the truth and be worried about hiding a few last skeletons in your closet. Once you drop all those bones and start heading down your life's path again, you get further and further away from them—unless you are still carrying any of them.

You can't forgive and then keep lying. You can't start again and have your marriage, your hearts, and your relationship be clean and white as snow if you are still holding onto anything that will place demands on you to lie again to cover it up. If you operate that way, years down the road it could crumble again.

If you mess up at work, your boss wants to hear the bad news quickly. He needs to hear it right away so together you can figure out damage control. So you can get the problem fixed. If you hide it, it grows. The longer it is hidden, the bigger the mess becomes.

Laine and I spent eighteen months in counseling before we had worked our new recipe into no-fail perfection. We were not perfect, but we knew the fresh ingredients, the right directions and the new utensils we now had could keep us cooking well for the rest of our lives.

We have stressed the importance of outside counseling a lot, but there are many utensils to help you put together a marital masterpiece. We strongly encourage you to get in real community with other couples with the same values. One of the biggest weapons the devil uses to split families apart is isolation. He gets everybody so busy and then so embroiled in their mess they don't spend time with anyone else on a regular basis. They don't open up and share what is really going on with anyone. They think they can handle it themselves. Or they are too tired and depressed to reach out. Isolation is a huge mistake in marriage.

We are created to connect. If you don't believe us, check out the book of Acts. It is the first book in the New Testament after Jesus was resurrected and went back to Heaven. It tells about the first Christians and how they lived and spread the stories of Jesus. They ate together, lived in community, shared everything. And when they did, the Bible says everyone's needs were met. Can you even imagine what that would look like? Today we have individual homes, jobs, cars, schools, and activities that keep us from simply living life together. We need to get back to some of that Acts way of life.

When you get into a group of ten to twelve people, you can open up in a safe place. You can really get to know each other. Be open. Become vulnerable. Build intimacy. Think of intimacy as this: into-me-you-see. Intimacy. It just means feeling close and allowing someone to get to know the real you. When you do, you will have friends to encourage you, check on you, hold you accountable, help with the kids, and listen when you need to talk.

Make sure these friends are for your marriage. Hanging out at clubs with singles will not help you revive your marriage. Having only single friends can make singleness look attractive. We are not saying you cannot have any single friends, but let's face it—they are not on the same life path you are and cannot relate.

Seek out couples who have been married longer than you have. Pick their brains about how they keep going, how they have overcome problems, and how they stay in love. Nothing beats experience. When you start to surround yourself with others who are determined to make their marriages thrive, you will be affirmed and encouraged that you are on the right path. And you will have people to pick you up, brush you off and point you back in the right direction if you get off track.

Another great utensil is knowledge. Get plugged into church where you can learn more about faith and God. Get some books on relationships, marriage, communication, the Bible, or something that interests both of you. If you are struggling with the kids, take a parenting course so you can get on the same page. If one of you does not like to read, see if the other spouse will read aloud for a few minutes each night. Get audiobooks and listen to them on drives. Put some podcasts or audiobooks on your audio player. Every time you learn something new, you add a new utensil to make your recipe just a little bit better.

Find an activity, hobby, sport or something you can do to have some fun together. Join a gym, take a cooking class, go to one of those painting places and create a work of art. It doesn't matter what you do. The point is to find something you can enjoy as a couple. When you sharpen your mind and your talents, you feel good about yourself. When you do it with the one you love, it brings out the best in both of you.

If you must work a lot to make ends meet, these goals may seem impossible. We are not saying you have to do all of this every day or every week if you just can't. But everyone can become intentional about carving out some sort of time to connect together. Find a moment or two to write a note and put it on the coffee pot, text a compliment or word of encouragement during the day, call just to say "hi," or take the first ten minutes when you both get home to walk outside or close your bedroom door and greet each other.

> "Everyone can become *intentional* about carving out some sort of time to connect together."

Ten minutes of "couch time" where you share about the day makes all the homework, dinner, bath times, and work you must get back to later in the evening seem easier. It's amazing how much easier all the mundane duties of life become when you feel like you are doing them as part of a team!

If you are still struggling to communicate civilly with each other, try this trick our counselor taught us. When we sat down together in our sessions, she would hand a rock to either me or Laine. The person with the rock was the one who got to speak. The other spouse could not interrupt or share their side until the rock got handed over. That helped us tremendously. For years, I felt like

Laine had cut me off whenever I tried to respond to anything she said. Most of the time, I gave up and quit trying to talk at all. Or I blew up and hurt her badly with nasty words. Try the rock trick. You can't talk until the rock is in your hands. When you have made your point, hand over the rock and listen to your spouse's side. It's a simple fix that can make a big improvement.

One more word: If you keep working and spending all your time running on empty, waiting for the right time to finally take that super vacation, it may never come. By the time it does, it probably will not meet your expectations anyway. When you pin all your hopes on one thing, chances are you will be disappointed. Work on the little things every day. Then if the big beach vacation comes your way, have a blast. If it doesn't, your relationship can create its own warm sunshine and summer fun.

If you ask me, I think there are a lot of false expectations we build into the idea of "dream" vacations. We plan and save and wait for the good times, instead of creating good times with each other in the daily tasks. I just like to be with Laine wherever I am most comfortable, whether it's on our own couch, in our room, or taking a walk outside.

If you were to ask my greatest day, my idea of the most fun I could have in my marriage, it's spending time with my wife and my three kids, eating a meal together and laughing about what we're all doing. Just enjoying each other's company. There is nothing sweeter than that. We had one of those times recently. Just fifteen minutes, sitting at our table and everyone was happy. It was heaven, perfection. No problems, just love. Laine and I looked at each other and looked at our three grown kids and I thought how much I loved everyone in that room and what a miracle it is that I have this.

Okay, so another tool, let's call it a knife in the butcher block that keeps your marriage sharp, is sex. If you are struggling in this area, get out of your comfort zone and talk about it. Make a plan to make it better, whether that means going to a doctor, improving your health, trying something new or learning more about how to please each other. In marriage, your bodies belong to each other. Sex can be an absolute reset button when things feel tough. Just the chemical release of endorphins and hormones make you feel better physically and emotionally. Did you know that an orgasm can open your sinuses? Seriously, sex in marriage should be the bomb. If your sex life is not, grab some new utensils (you can interpret that however you like, as long as you both are okay with it) and start playing around in the kitchen.

Laine and I are naturally very independent. So when we come together, it reminds us of how we are to be united. We can be way overwhelmed and way stressed out, and sex helps us reconnect and relax.

(Hey kids, if you are reading this, you can skip this next paragraph.)

Now, every time we do it, it's different. We keep looking at each other and saying, "That was the best it has ever been." And we just said that the last time. Sex cannot be used to fulfill the husband's manhood. A husband should not view his wife as a sexual object but as a treasure to be cherished and valued. Likewise, sex should not be used as a bargaining tool by the wife. She should not with-hold it so she can feel powerful. It is a full expression of love, a gift to each other that should be shared, and shared often.

When Laine and I added all the new utensils in this chapter to our no-fail recipe for a revived marriage, they were mainly utensils that helped us do the basics better. Your utensils don't have to be all fancy icing tips and lemon zesters, things you stick in a drawer and have to think twice to remember what they are when you see them. Your new utensils may be more like spatulas, pizza cutters, and chip clips. Smiles and hugs that scoop you off the pan when you are feeling overdone, little notes to slice up your day into more manageable pieces, and moments of fun that hold your marriage together and keep it from getting stale.

Over and over, the Bible talks about living in the truth. That's definitely one of the most important utensils. There should be no doubt now that the truth will set you free. If you are a liar, you will never have anything good and of value.

My best tools that I use every day for all things start the moment I wake up in the morning. I say to myself, "Today, I walk forward in and with absolute truth and without any fear." I also ask the Lord, "Lord, what can I do for you today?" These two tools empower you and help you conquer any obstacle or challenge.

I may not know what I am doing for the day or how it will go, as I must leave the actions and the outcomes in God's hands, but in more than ten years now of starting my days with these declarations, I have gone from having mostly bad days with an occasional good day to good days with the occasional bad. Adding absolute truth serves to remove fear, a nice bonus. If you are completely honest, you never have to look over your shoulder. You're never afraid someone might "find out" anything. Plus, allowing God to direct your path toward His outcome makes life easier and grander than anything I ever achieved through my own efforts.

Use the Right Utensils: Our No-Fail Recipe

INGREDIENTS:

1 married couple

1 Christian counselor

A bunch of Christian friends

1 solid church

Tank of gas and a car to get to the store

Whatever ingredients you like

UTENSILS:

Any utensils to help you cook some very fine fare, including but not limited to:

Spatula

Apple corer

Grater

Pizza cutter

Cooking Shears

Icing Tips

DIRECTIONS:

Take one married couple and have them choose a great Christian counselor. Attend sessions faithfully. Find a solid church and a close group of friends. Then get in the car and drive to the store. Browse the kitchen section, allowing each spouse to choose any new utensils they want to try. Take them home and cook up some new connections. Have fun!

Use the Right Utensils:
Our No-Fail Recipe Card

From the Kitchen of: _____

INGREDIENTS:

_____

_____

_____

_____

_____

_____

_____

DIRECTIONS:

_____

_____

_____

_____

_____

_____

_____

_____

_____

Meringues

INGREDIENTS:

4 egg whites, at room temperature

Pinch of salt

1 cup superfine sugar

1/2 teaspoon vanilla extract

FOR BEST RESULTS:

Don't make meringues on a rainy or humid day, it will leave them flat. Eggs that are 3 or 4 days old produce fluffier Meringues.

Cold eggs separate more easily, so separate first, then bring to room temperature. Warmer egg whites whip faster and fluffier. Usually 30 minutes is adequate to obtain room temperature.

The tiniest bit of egg yolk will wreck a meringue, so use caution when separating. Also, avoid letting your fingers come in contact with the egg whites.

I like to use superfine sugar when making meringue because it dissolves faster than table sugar.

Once you start a making Meringues, continue it straight through. Do not stop. Copper, stainless-steel, or glass bowls work best. Plastic bowls prevent the whites from getting stiff.

Make sure your utensils are immaculately clean, grease-free, and completely dry. Meringues don't like any moisture. Avoid leaving oils from your hands on the utensils you just washed.

DIRECTIONS:

Place egg whites into a large bowl and beat with an electric mixer on medium speed or with a rotary beater until egg whites form peaks with tips that curl over when the beaters are lifted.

Gradually add sugar a few spoonfuls at a time, beating the whole time. DO NOT add sugar before whipping the egg whites. Adding sugar at the beginning can double the whipping time. Add sugar at the end when the whites have formed soft peaks.

The batter is ready when it is not runny and you can hold a spoonful upside down and none of it drops off. When you swirl a spoon through it and the swirls hold their shape indefinitely.

Fill a quart-size plastic bag (or pastry bag fitted with a 1/2-inch plain tip) with the meringue batter. Seal the bag, leaving a small opening for air to escape as you squeeze. Cut off 1 corner of the bag, making an opening 3/4-inch-wide. Gently push batter down and pipe into 1 1/2-inch-diameter cookies onto parchment-lined baking sheets, spacing 1/2 inch apart.

Bake at 200 degrees for 1 1/2 hours, until dry and crisp throughout. Transfer to wire racks and let the meringues cool to room temperature on baking sheets, about 15 minutes.

NOTE FROM LAINE AND STEVE:

This recipe takes just the right everything, from the bowl to the temperature of the eggs. Meringues can be tough to whip into shape, and your marriage may feel the same way for a while. Don't give up! The sweet lightness that comes at the end is simply satisfying.

CHAPTER EIGHT

Bake, Simmer, or Stew

Taking Time to Improve

"Cooking is an art and patience a virtue... Careful shopping, fresh ingredients and an unhurried approach are nearly all you need."
Keith Floyd

"Patience was not something that came naturally to me, but in cooking it is the quintessential skill."
Gail Simmons

I love the kitchen. I love to cook. A bunch of fresh vegetables, a good-looking cut of meat, and herbs and spices all lined up on the kitchen counter inspire me. Give me eggs, butter, milk, flour, sugar, baking powder, and a few other goodies and I will bake a

143

mean cake. I am happy to create things that taste good and nourish my family. I love to make meals so we can gather together around the table and connect.

If you are applying this no-fail recipe to revive your marriage, you are nourishing the most important relationship you will ever have in this life. You will be feeding the heart and soul of your spouse, and they will be feeding yours. Once you have assembled all the right ingredients and put them together, you have to trust in the cooking process.

Think about all the ingredients for a great cake. Eggs. Milk. Butter. Sugar. Oil, butter or shortening. Vanilla. Flour. Baking powder. Individually, I would not want to eat any of those raw ingredients. Even when you first cream the butter, sugar, and eggs together, it still doesn't look or taste like much. When you get the batter all ready, it tastes pretty good, but the raw eggs can make you sick. Only when you pour it in the pan and pop it in the oven does that batter become what it was meant to be. The baking process transforms the whole creation. You can't get a cake out of batter without applying the heat.

> ## "You can't get a cake out of batter without applying the *heat*."

As the batter meets the high temperatures in the oven, the baking powder produces tiny bubbles of gas which make the cake rise up light and fluffy. Protein in the egg hardens, which makes the cake firm. Butter, oil, or shortening keep the cake from becoming dry and crumbly. When the baking time is up, the batter has disappeared and a beautiful cake remains in its place.

When you gather together the fresh quality ingredients for a full transformation in your marriage, you have to apply the heat.

You must allow time to bake, simmer, or stew. It's in the cooking process that the chemistry occurs. I know you've heard the old expression, "If you can't stand the heat, get out of the kitchen." Well, we're telling you that you need to take the heat, bask in it, and stay in your kitchen until your newly revived relationship comes out of the oven and fills your home with the wonderful smells of reconciliation, such as love, peace, and joy.

Think of it this way. It took time for your marriage to get to the desperate place it was in when you picked up this book. It took years for Steve and me to become so miserable together we hated each other. For us, it was about seventeen years, in fact. We needed to shed those years of baggage that had been weighing us down, years of bad habits in communication, harsh tones, and just plain rudeness to each other.

We experienced a complete turnaround in our attitudes right at the beginning when we made a promise to start again from scratch. And we believe every couple can experience the same miracle in an instant of softened hearts and a willingness to start again. But from that miracle moment you have to create a whole new life together. That's the cooking process. We challenge you to give your new marriage at least one month of "cooking time" for every one year you were unhappy together.

For Steve and me, that meant seventeen months of baking new habits like dating each other, counseling, and talking to each other civilly. We had to preheat the oven of our marriage with those very first date nights, warm it up by passing the rock back and forth and letting each spouse talk, and finally bake it over time by changing our words and actions. That timeframe was just about right. We finished our season of counseling after eighteen months. By then, our marriage looked and smelled totally, completely different than anything we had put together in the past. We were ready to have our cake and eat it too.

Before Laine and I revived our marriage, we could not have preheated anything. Our emotional ovens either wouldn't heat up at all, leaving us acting cold as ice toward each other, or they were constantly set to broil, meaning we burned up everything we touched. There was no slowly getting to the right temperature, no baking process so we could form anything that smelled and tasted good. All we knew how to make in our marriage was a mess.

Looking back now on the process we went through to fully restore our partnership, I can see how well cooking analogies fit. Because when we applied the correct heat over time to our relationship, not too emotionally hot or cold, the result was something wonderful I will enjoy for the rest of my days.

Laine may have compared the whole thing to baking a cake, but I'm going to talk about the meat and potatoes. A slab of meat is made up of minerals, fat, water, and protein. The protein molecules in the meat are bonded together in tight coils. When you apply heat to those proteins, those molecular ties begin to break and the coils start to unwind. The water in the meat begins to leach out and evaporate, and the fat liquefies somewhat and flavors the cut. Can't you just picture a juicy steak grilling? Can you almost smell it?

When we applied the right heat over time—by which I mean continuously, day-by-day, dedicating ourselves to put into practice all the new things we were learning and trying—the tightly wound coils in our hearts began to unwind. The fears, insecurities, mistrust, and anger melted like the fat sizzling over the flames. Some of the extra water, like too many hours on the job, too many commitments, and too much time away from each other leached out and left us with a beautifully seared marriage. A flavorful, juicy cut you could sink your teeth into.

As you apply the "heat" of the changes we have recommended in your marriage, your old bad habits, faulty communication, and irritation will begin to uncoil. It takes time, but the end result is more than worth it.

Think of your marriage as a pot on the stove you want to simmer. When you simmer something, you cook it in liquid at a temperature just below the boiling point. Simmering allows small bubbles of delicious aroma to escape but does not reach the point where rolling waves of bubbles are continuously breaking across the surface.

Simmering is gentler than boiling, and it requires constant tending and stirring to keep the ingredients cooking together without breaking into pieces or drying out. When you poach fish, you simmer it to keep it from falling apart. When you simmer meat, it remains fork-tender. Boiling meat can overheat those proteins and make them tough. Simmering is also used to get the fats released from the meat to float to the top of a stock so you can remove them easily and keep the stock clear.

If you boil green vegetables for a brief amount of time, the high heat helps them keep their color. They bump up against each other briefly but never meld. When you simmer ingredients, they fold into each other again and again, softening over time and taking on each other's flavors.

When Laine and I reached the boiling point and stayed there, our marriage became so dry and tough we could not swallow even one more bite. Remember when you were real little and you took a bite of meat and chewed and chewed that sucker but it just got dryer and dryer in your mouth? Eventually, it felt so big and so dry you could not swallow any of it. You either gagged and choked or spit it back out on your plate. Marriages on constant boil or broil are just not appetizing to anybody.

If we had taken all of the counselor's advice and tried to cram the new conversations, activities, and daily tasks into a few days and call our new recipe done, it would have been either way underdone or we would have had to dial up the heat so high we would be right back in the middle of more conflict. The best things in life just take time, and there is no getting around it. Remember that one of the fruits of the Spirit is patience. Not the most fun fruit to take a bite of, but there you go. It's right there on the list, which means God wants us to apply it to our marriages too.

Laine will never forget, or let me forget, my reaction to her body when she was still in the hospital the day after giving birth to our firstborn. Her stomach was still so swollen I asked the doctor if he was sure there wasn't another baby still in there. And I was totally serious! Her belly still looked very pregnant, and neither of us had expected that. We did not know the uterus requires time to shrink back down. It takes months for that muscle to lose all the extra elasticity it acquired to hold a full-term baby. When Laine left the hospital, she still looked six or seven months pregnant. Really, she didn't look too much different than when we went in to have the baby.

Everything was different though. Now we had our sweet little boy to take home with us, a new life we had created together. Your new marriage may still look swollen, maybe even unappealing to you for a while, its muscles all stretched out. Keep in mind no matter what it looks like, changes have occurred. Healing is taking place. There is new life in your marriage, precious new life and habits you need to take care of around the clock. Nurture those new ways of communicating, those tender feelings, until the old muscles shrink back to their proper shape and size and the new life grows and thrives. It takes exercising new ways of thinking and behaving over time for your relationship to look and feel beautiful again.

Okay, I don't really hold that story against my sweet Steve. Mostly, I just laugh and shake my head as I think back on what young, naive kids we were when we thought we could start these things called marriage and family and make them a success. There was so much we didn't know about how our pasts had shaped us, how circumstances would try us, and how our emotional baggage could wound us. We were like vegetables bouncing around in a boiling pot, always under pressure and bubbling over.

Nowadays, I really prefer to make stews, roasts, and other things I can simmer and stew. When you take a slow cooker and put a roast in it or some stew meat that you have browned, then add some stock or vegetable juice and throw in some cut potatoes, carrots, and onions, you can simmer those for hours and the delightful smell starts to permeate the entire house. The juices from the meat blend with the stock or juice, and the starch from the potatoes thickens the whole mixture just a bit. The carrots and onions soften and sweeten the whole dish. After a few hours, each ingredient in your stew has shared its flavor with the rest of the dish.

When your marriage cooks over time on a nice, slow simmer, all of your best qualities complement each other. No longer are you separate ingredients bouncing and clashing off each other in a boil or floating limply around each other in a pot with no heat. When you sit and stew (in a good way), you realize you were not that far apart in the first place, no matter how emotionally distant you may have become.

Steve and I fell in love because our core values and goals in life were much the same. We wanted the same things out of life; we just had very different external expressions and ways of getting what we wanted. During the worst times of our marriage, I thought we were miles apart. We had nothing in common that I could see.

Underneath, however, Steve was the same man he had been all along. I was the same girl he had fallen in love with. Our biggest problem was not being too different. No, our biggest issue was that we did not know how to express our feelings in healthy ways. We had created so much emotional distance between us we could no longer recognize how close we really were on the inside. When the layers of hurt and anger were peeled away like the outer leaves of an artichoke, when the disappointment and miscommunication were pulled out like the thorny inner leaves, only then could we scoop out the fuzz of distrust and finally uncover our true hearts to each other again.

When all of the garbage was gone and our hearts were exposed, we discovered we were still the same at our core as we were in the beginning. We wanted to love God, each other, and our children well. We desired to build a lifetime and a legacy together. We still looked forward to sitting on a big front porch one day, rocking our grandchildren. Once we mixed the right ingredients together and began slow cooking them over time, our marriage began to simmer right along.

"When all of the garbage was gone and our hearts were *Exposed*, we discovered we were still the same at our core as we were in the beginning."

One of the biggest benefits of reviving your marriage over time is the opportunity to break what we are going to call "generational curses" in your family line. Now we are not trying to sound all mystic or New Age or crazy charismatic or anything. We simply mean that there are bad habits, emotionally crippling behaviors, addictions and other issues that can devastate your life that may have been running themes along the branches of your family tree.

Maybe you, your mother and your grandmother have struggled with depression. Maybe your grandpa, your uncle, your brother, and you battle inner rage. Whatever the problems are, if you have an issue that shows up again and again in your family line, we would call that a "generational curse." It's an area of sin in your lives that seems to be passed on from generation to generation.

The good news is that by surrendering your lives to Jesus and following His call to revive your marriage, you get a brand new opportunity to break those chains of mental illness, addiction, or emotional baggage. Your children can become free. Your grandchildren can become free. Four generations of unwed teen moms in your family? Pray every day for your children to keep their sexual purity and not to become teen parents.

As a child of the King of Kings, you have authority over evil. You have the right to tell it to go away in Jesus' name. Romans 8:11 says, "The Spirit of God, who raised Jesus from the dead, lives in you. And just as God raised Christ Jesus from the dead, he will give life to your mortal bodies by this same Spirit living within you." (NLT)

That's pretty exciting. Think about that. We have the same power inside of us that brought a dead man back to life. Surely that means we can use some of that power to banish our bad habits, stop our self-destructive tendencies, and destroy the addictions that want to take down our family legacy.

One other cooking process we did not touch on in this chapter involves marinating. When you take fish and marinate it in citrus juices, it makes a dish called *ceviche*. Even though heat has not been applied, when the seafood spends time soaking in the lime or other citrus juices, the acid "cooks" the meat. When we marinate ourselves in the Word of God, pouring it over and into our lives on a daily basis, we allow His flavor to penetrate our tough tissues and issues. Only God can fully restore and revive not only our relationship in marriage, but also our children, our grandchildren, and all the future branches of our family tree.

Wouldn't that be a great testimony in this me-first culture filled with broken marriages and family dysfunction? If you could point at your family tree and show all the branches intact, what a witness that would be to the power of God's love for you and your love for each other. When you slow cook your new marriage over time, you achieve a no-fail recipe that can be handed down and repeated for generations to come. Delicious!

Bake, Simmer or Stew: Our No-Fail Recipe

INGREDIENTS:

1 newly revived marriage
3 cups of the stock of new habits
2 cups better communication
2 tablespoons trust
5 cups patience

DIRECTIONS:

Turn the marital slow cooker on simmer. Too hot, and the couple will boil. Too cold, and the best of both will not blend.

Add the newly revived marriage to the warmed pot, along with the stock of new habits, cups of better communication and diced tablespoons of trust and lots of patience. Put the lid on the slow cooker and allow all the ingredients to simmer together over time.

Best served hot when all the ingredients are tender and the flavors have joined together.

Bake, Simmer or Stew:
Our No-Fail Recipe Card

From the Kitchen of: _____

INGREDIENTS:

_____

_____

_____

_____

_____

_____

_____

DIRECTIONS:

_____

_____

_____

_____

_____

_____

_____

_____

_____

Slow Stewed Chicken

INGREDIENTS:

1 (1-ounce) envelope taco seasoning

6 boneless, skinless chicken breasts

1 (16-ounce) jar salsa

DIRECTIONS:

Dump all ingredients into a slow cooker and stir. Cook low 6 to 8 hours. When done, chicken should shred easily with a fork.

For tacos, serve with flour tortillas, guacamole, lettuce, shredded cheese and sour cream. Use leftover chicken for soup.

TORTILLA SOUP:

2 cups leftover shredded chicken

1/2 large yellow onion, chopped

32 ounces chicken broth

2 handfuls chopped cilantro

Juice from 1 lime

1 (14-ounce) can each: corn, diced tomatoes, diced tomatoes with chiles, and black beans

2 to 3 tablespoons tomato paste

2 teaspoons each: cumin, chili powder, and garlic powder

Dump everything in a pot and simmer about 30 minutes. Garnish with cheese and crispy tortilla strips!

Slow Stewed Chicken

NOTE FROM LAINE AND STEVE:

We chose this recipe because stewing enhances the flavors of this tasty dish and because you get not just one meal, but two. When you make your marriage better, you can cook up new ways to love each other out of the same ingredients and share your success with others too.

NOTES:

_____

_____

_____

_____

_____

_____

_____

_____

_____

_____

_____

_____

_____

_____

_____

_____

When the Soufflé Falls
Surviving Setbacks

"Cooking requires confident guesswork and improvisation—experimentation and substitution, dealing with failure and uncertainty in a creative way."
Paul Theroux

"For the world was built to develop character, and we must learn that the setbacks and grieves which we endure help us in our marching onward."
Henry Ford

*S*top! Please don't put this book down yet. If you feel a little overwhelmed, a little discouraged even, don't quit now. If you and your spouse have offered and received true forgiveness, you should be experiencing enough warmth that your marital oven is at least on preheat again. If it is not, the great thing about life is that as long as you are breathing, you can keep trying. I love Lamentations 3:22-23, which says, "The Lord's love never ends; his mercies never stop. They are new every morning; Lord, your loyalty is great." (NCV)

Isn't that awesome? That means whatever happened in the past is gone; you don't have to dwell on it. Whatever is going on right now will also pass. If you and your spouse are not getting along today, if you can't find the right ingredients or utensils to make your marriage better, tomorrow is another day. With God on your side you get a clean, fresh start every morning. What wonderful news!

> "The great thing about life is that as long as you are *breathing*, you can keep trying."

So if you are slipping back into old bad habits, tired of waiting for feelings to rekindle, or having doubts this whole no-fail recipe thing can really revive your marriage, then start again—again. Turn back to chapters two and three and read them one more time. Take your mistakes before God and offer them to Him. Confess anything left over and get it out in the open. Look right in each other's eyes and ask to start again from scratch. Go put yourself in the middle of some trusted friends who will help you keep you remarriage simmering. It is absolutely certain you will have setbacks. But in God's kitchen, you get right back up and start cooking again.

> "The godly may trip seven times, but they will get up again. But one disaster is enough to overthrow the wicked."—Proverbs 24:16 (NLT)

Jesus offered do-overs throughout his ministry on earth. Remember the Samaritan woman who met Him at the well in John 4? Jesus told her she could drink living water that would keep her from ever being thirsty again. He then revealed to her that He was the Messiah. He told the woman all about herself, that she had been married five times and was currently living with a man who was not her husband. She was so overcome she went and spread the news to everyone in town about the things Jesus had told her. The result? She was forgiven and used by God to bring others to meet Jesus and believe in Him as the Son of God who came to save the world.

What was so wild about this story is that in ancient times, people didn't get do-overs. Forgiveness was unheard of. It was literally an "eye for an eye" in most of the regions. Think about the bloodthirsty Romans who sent people to the Coliseum to fight to the death. Think about the Arab countries who live even today under Islamic law. If you stole something back then and sometimes now, your hand was cut off. If you committed adultery or murder, you paid with your own life.

When Jesus came, He taught people to forgive again and again. In Matthew 18:21-22, the disciple Peter asks Him about forgiveness.

> "At that point Peter got up the nerve to ask, 'Master, how many times do I forgive a brother or sister who hurts me? Seven?' Jesus replied, 'Seven! Hardly. Try seventy times seven.'" (THE MESSAGE)

The point Jesus was trying to make was not to count all the ways your spouse has offended you until you get to 490 times and then start holding grudges if they tick you off after that. What Christ wanted to get across is that forgiveness should be offered in unlimited supply. That can be so tough to do when someone hurts you repeatedly. However, each time you offer forgiveness you clean out your own heart. You do not condone the wrong done to you, but you refuse to allow it to have any power over your heart and your emotions.

Restoration is a process. You will have lots of times when one of you says something that triggers those old, nasty habits and emotions. Suddenly, you will feel like nothing has changed at all. Don't listen to those old tapes. Things *have* changed. Your marriage is on a new path. But your old communication patterns and thought processes took a long time to become ingrained in you. Give your restoration time too. Bad days will inevitably get mixed in there with the good ones. The goal is to keep putting a new batch of ingredients on to cook every time you burn up the old ones. Keep fighting for more good days, and the bad ones will become less and less frequent.

> "Let us not become weary in doing good, for at the proper time we will reap a harvest if we do not give up."—Galatians 6:9 (NIV)

Don't grow weary in the cooking process. Remember, fresh ingredients combined with the right directions, using the proper utensils and cooked at the right temperature over time will produce a feast for a lifetime.

The area Laine and I probably struggled in the most was our words. God spoke the world into existence. With the power of the Holy Spirit in you, you can speak new life into your marriage. On the other hand, you can also speak death over it. Over the first seventeen years, we spoke a lot of death into our relationship.

> *"Words kill, words give life; they're either poison or fruit—you choose."—Proverbs 18:21 (MSG)*

One way to counteract the damage your tongue can do is to write down what you want in your relationship and find Bible verses that match these desires. Post the goals and the verses on notecards or slips of paper or even sticky notes on your bathroom mirrors, your coffee pot, your steering wheel, anywhere you will see them regularly. Say these goals and verses out loud every time you see them. Speak life into your dreams, your feelings, your goals for your marriage. Then speak God's life into it with His Word.

This powerful combination can bring about huge changes in your marriage. When you feel discouraged about your progress, put yourselves in time-out from your problems and grab a piece of paper and a pen or your tablets or cell phones and write down a list of where you want to be together in one month, one year, one decade.

"Speak life into your *dreams*, your feelings, your goals for your marriage. Then speak God's life into it with His Word."

Visualize yourself together in old age. What will you be doing? Rocking grandkids on the porch like we hope to be doing? Will you be in the mountains? On a beach? Taking cruises or helping others on missions trips? Will you be opening your own business or retiring from the one you have now?

Start making a plan to turn those dreams into reality. Do something that makes you feel like you are investing in your future. Visit a travel agent. Go to an RV show. Open a savings account for the special occasion you are dreaming of. You can't fail or lose the battle unless you quit. Don't let setbacks conquer your success.

I think you have to remember that marriage is like a marathon, and every setback is like the wall runners hit when they feel they cannot take even one more step. If runners push just one step past the wall, they get a "runner's high" that gives them a second wind to make it across the finish line. Their fatigue and exhaustion disappear, and they actually feel better than they did near the beginning of the race.

If you are hitting your wall, just tell yourself to take one more step. Do or say one more nice thing for your spouse. Hang in there one more minute, hour, or day. Smile, pray, forgive, talk, and love with your words and actions just a little bit more. When you see the finish line, it will all be worth it.

Before I really understood the power my words had and the damage they were doing, I was constantly being negative. I used to look at Steve so harshly, so negatively. I used to hate everything he did. Now, he is still doing a lot of those same things but I find value in them. I think I learned how to turn it around through one simple illustration. You can try it too.

Take a sheet of blank white paper and an ink pen. Put a tiny dot of ink in the middle of that paper. If your spouse is generally a good-hearted person and you know he or she is not acting with malice toward you all the time, then think of all the things they do wrong as that little ink spot. All the rest of the paper, all the white part, is the good things your spouse is actually trying to do. What you are seeing as wrong most of the time may just be different than the way you would do it. It's not right or wrong; the end result is often the same.

There are many roads you can take to get to the same location. Sure, some of them have more lights, a lower speed limit, or more traffic. Maybe you like to zoom right to your destination. Perhaps your spouse is a sightseer, more apt to hit the lights in order to see the sights along the way. Does it really matter as long as you end up at the same destination?

Take a look at all the things that irritate you in a day or a week about your spouse. Now look at all the things your spouse has done for you, your kids, or your family this week. Did she work long hours at a job? Did he clean the house? Did either of you run the kids around? Did you help with homework, fix a meal, or put oil or gas in the car? All of the mundane, tiresome, daily duties and tasks should count for something in each other's eyes. Do not overlook the daily. Thank and praise each other for these little things. Because it is often not the things we are doing or not doing for each other. It's our attitude and our perspective. It's our hearts.

Change your hearts and you can be happy every day of your life.

When I changed my heart toward Steve, instead of nagging at him all the time about working, I thought what a great husband I had who would work so hard and so much for us. Steve was doing the same thing—working. I chose to look at his work positively instead of negatively. That was the only difference. But what a different it made in our relationship.

"Do not overlook the *daily*. Thank and praise each other for these little things."

Practice saying positive things like that to yourself, to your spouse, and about your marriage. Let go of the little things that are unimportant in the big picture. Praise each other instead of finding fault. Praise God together that your marriage is being revived. Praise Him for the gift of His forgiveness and the way He showed you how to forgive each other.

Keep reminding yourself feelings do not have to line up right away with your actions. Emotions are fickle. They lie. They betray us. You can go days, months, or years without feeling "in love" with your spouse. Then in just a few days, with the right words and actions, you can fall head over heels for the same person all over again.

A very good friend of mine learned that crucial lesson from her Aunt Jamie. Aunt Jamie and Uncle Larry were married for more than twenty-five years and had three grown children when Jamie fell smack out of love with Larry. They had always had very different interests and did not spend a whole lot of time together once they became empty nesters.

Jamie was a social butterfly. She acted in local community theater productions and found joy in going to the local donut shop every morning and chatting with everyone who stopped by. She made friends everywhere she went. She also loved to collect things as much as she collected people. She shopped at Goodwill often and adored passing on the bargains she found. One time, Jamie bought a knickknack for her sister Jeri because it looked like something Jeri would love. Turns out, her sister had donated that item to that very Goodwill store. Jamie bought back the trinket Jeri had given away in the first place.

Larry, on the other hand, was a homebody. He liked nothing more than to sit in his chair and watch television. He never said much. He was a loner without friends, hobbies, or many activities. Larry did not like to go out. He did not care about collecting things. He did not like to shop, find bargains, or pass them on.

Larry did not share Jamie's faith either. He was a self-proclaimed atheist. Jamie loved Jesus. Yet Jamie had taken Larry as her husband all those years ago and wanted to make her remaining years good ones with the man she had promised to love for life.

"I fell completely out of love with Larry," Jamie told her niece (my good friend). "But I knew I was supposed to stay married to him. I prayed, 'Lord, please let me fall in love with Larry again. Please let me fall in love with my husband.' I prayed that multiple times a day, every day. It took two years of praying that prayer before it was answered. Two long, dry years during which I really wanted to leave. I did not like my life with Larry at all. But I kept praying. One day, I looked at my husband and it was like my eyes were opened. All the feelings of being in love with Larry washed over me again. I felt like a teenager. I fell madly in love with my own husband again."[1]

Larry had not changed a bit. Jamie's circumstances had not changed. She still liked to be upbeat and bubbly, a Tigger to Larry's Eeyore if you know your Winnie the Pooh characters. Still, God honored Jamie's faithfulness by rekindling her heart's fire for her husband. Jamie kept loving Jesus and Larry for more than another decade before she died. By loving Larry faithfully, over time she was able to draw him out more. In the last years of Jamie's life, the couple loved to go to breakfast together, took a trip or two, and enjoyed each other's company.

Starting again from scratch is a beautiful opportunity, because it gives you a future with the one you started marriage with in the first place. And when setbacks come, which they most certainly will, you just tell yourself you'll have a better day tomorrow.

> **"Starting again from *scratch* gives you a future with the one you started marriage with in the first place."**

That's what Steve and I did just recently. We had both been traveling a lot. We were overtired and had not connected much. Then we had an argument one night over something silly, I'm sure. Whatever it was, we just could not see eye-to-eye. I decided to go to bed. Now I know it is best not to go to bed angry, but when I headed up the stairs I was frustrated and out of sorts with my husband. I know he felt the same way about me. Once I got upstairs, I took out my cell phone and texted Steve.

"Maybe we will have a better day tomorrow, right, Bear?" I typed.

"Yes, we certainly will," my knight in slightly dented armor replied.

That little text was enough to give us hope for our future. It didn't solve whatever it was we argued about. But it didn't matter. Looking forward to the next day when we could start again gave us just enough light to take the next step with each other. It reminded us once again that although we can be very different people in our communication and expression, we are always on the same team.

Until we die, Steve and I will be fallible human beings who say hurtful things in times of temper or terror or tiredness. But we know for sure that we are now ultimately for each other, not against each other. That means when something hurtful comes, we can toss it out and start cooking again.

Okay, now I am going to talk about something that could be more than a setback. It could be the one area that causes your marriage to be so burnt in the bottom of the pot you have to throw the whole thing out. I'm talking about allowing others into your marriage. Not just outright affairs, but also flirting, exchanging numbers, doing lunches or allowing an attraction to build between you and any other person than your spouse.

We are just going to acknowledge right here that you can, in fact, be attracted to others when you are married. And others will almost undoubtedly be attracted to you. The key to preserving the love in your marriage is not to put yourself in places where flirting is the norm (Going to bars and clubs without your spouse should be an automatic red flag.) and not to allow any fleeting attraction to take hold when it comes your way.

Okay, Husband. Let's say you are at a business lunch and a pretty woman at another table is staring at you. When you feel that stare and glance over, she smiles. Here's where you nip it in the bud. Either turn away or smile a disinterested smile. No warm smile, no inviting smile. Just a polite dismissal. What you definitely do not do is get up and go introduce yourself. You do not tell yourself she might make a good client or that you are just being friendly. Turn away and pray for strength to resist any temptation.

Sure, it feels good to be noticed. It's a turn-on. But let's follow the wrong action through in our imagination. You get up, walk over and introduce yourself, and then what? You go out. She either 1) falls in love with you but you can't be with her full-time so you break up and she calls your wife, or 2) gets mad at you or doesn't fall in love with you and so you break up and ... she calls your wife. Unless she doesn't know your name, she is going to, one day soon, call your wife. Either way, this scenario ends in disaster.

Keep the pot cooking at home and you don't need any other dishes. Believe me when I tell you that the wife of your youth can give you more than any flirtation ever could.

"Keep the pot cooking at *home* and you don't need any other dishes."

Wife, when an attractive man makes an appointment with you at the office or comes to fix something at your house, consider turning him over to someone else or remain in another room while repairs are being made. The devil wants to destroy your marriage, and he will flatter you through the attention of others. Picture that cute repairman with big ugly nose hairs or something. Whatever will allow you to take any stray thought captive and dismiss this guy pronto.

Don't undress a stranger in your imagination. Don't fool your-selves into thinking it's okay to watch porn together. Don't read novels or watch movies filled with graphic sex scenes either. Sex is reserved for the two of you, to bring you together as one. It is designed to make you closer to each other than anyone else, to bring you pleasure and delight, to relieve stress and tension and help your love grow. Treat it as holy.

When people say their marriage is over, they mean they are quitting. Quitters are losers. You need to look at your marriage as a game of chess, not poker. You are not in it to win the pot all for yourself or to fold. If you are in a tough season in your marriage, you have just made a bad move on the chess board. You can strategize and move your pieces until you are in a better position and your marriage is no longer in jeopardy. If quitting is not an option, then it is your job to make those moves and get your marriage to another season.

"When people say their *marriage* is over, they mean they are quitting."

Maybe that means noticing when your wife is tired and needs a break and taking her out to dinner instead of asking her what there is to eat. Even better, ask her where she wants to go eat. Make it an occasion by making the plan. Maybe it means giving your husband a pass instead of rising to the occasion for a fight the next time he snaps at you. Instead, gently ask him if he is okay and if you can do anything for him. When you hurt each other, apply the bandages of gentleness and kindness until you heal each other again.

Every day is brand new, and you don't have to bring any of the old into it. God gives us that every morning. Every morning I make the decision to get out of bed, put my feet on the ground, and walk forward in the truth with no fear. I ask God to lead me minute by minute. All day long, I try to do what God tells me to do. When God puts something in my path, I go where He leads. You can't lose your marriage as long as you start fresh every day.

Your marriage can make it as long as you keep fighting for the success of it because you never "get there." You are never at the end. Good or bad, right this minute you can keep trying. There is no "over," only do-overs, unless you get divorced. God gives you the free will to decide when it's over. But the fresh opportunities to try again are not exhausted until you die. Your marriage does not have to be over until God calls you home.

When the Soufflé Falls: Our No-Fail Recipe

INGREDIENTS:

1 partially revived couple
A heaping handful of setbacks
Positive thoughts and words, to taste
6 cups of do-overs
A lifetime of new morning mercies

DIRECTIONS:

Take the partially revived couple and toss in the handful of setbacks. Watch the marriage begin to fade as frustrations and flirtations try to turn it into a mess.

Fold in positive thoughts and words posted where the couple can see them and say them aloud regularly, to taste.

Stir in 6 cups of do-overs every time a mistake is made. Add more if needed.

Start again from scratch with new mercies every morning to create the best batch of this dish for the rest of your life.

When the Soufflé Falls:
Our No-Fail Recipe Card

From the Kitchen of: _____

INGREDIENTS:

_____

_____

_____

_____

_____

_____

_____

DIRECTIONS:

_____

_____

_____

_____

_____

_____

_____

_____

_____

Kahlua Chocolate Soufflé

Makes 8 servings

INGREDIENTS

3 tablespoons plus 2/3 cup sugar, divided

2 tablespoons Kahlua

2 teaspoons instant espresso powder

1/3 cup unsweetened Dutch-process cocoa powder, sifted

1 1/2 cups low-fat milk

2 tablespoons unsalted butter

2 tablespoons canola oil

1/4 cup white whole-wheat flour, or all-purpose flour

4 large egg yolks at room temperature

8 large egg whites at room temperature

1/8 teaspoon salt

DIRECTIONS:

Position rack in lower third of oven; preheat to 375 degrees. Coat 8 (10-ounce) ramekins or a 2 1/2-quart soufflé dish with cooking spray. Coat with 3 tablespoons sugar by tilting to evenly distribute; tap out excess. Place on a baking sheet.

Combine Kahlua and espresso powder until dissolved. Stir in remaining 2/3 cup sugar and cocoa powder.

Heat milk in a small saucepan over medium heat until steaming. Melt butter and oil in a medium saucepan over medium-low heat. Whisk in flour and cook, whisking, for 2 minutes. Slowly whisk in hot milk, and cook over medium-low heat, whisking, until mixture is the consistency of thick batter, 2 to 4 minutes. Transfer to a large bowl. Whisk in egg yolks, one at a time, until incorporated. Whisk in Kahlua mixture.

Clean and dry a large mixing bowl and beaters, making sure there are no traces of oil. (Any oil may prevent your soufflé from rising properly.) Beat egg whites in the bowl with electric mixer on medium speed until foamy. Add salt; gradually increase speed to high, and beat until shiny and stiff, but not dry. Do not overbeat—stop when egg whites hold their shape in the bowl and on the beater but don't look overly dry or lumpy.

Using a rubber spatula, stir 1/3 of the whites into egg-yolk mixture. Fold in remaining egg whites just until distributed. It's OK if a few streaks remain. Spoon into prepared dish(es).

Bake until puffed and firm, 20 to 24 minutes for ramekins, 38 to 42 minutes for soufflé dish. (Resist the temptation to peek— an open oven door will let in cool air and interrupt rising.)

Once out of the oven, even a beautifully puffed soufflé will slowly deflate, so go directly to the table to show off its beauty, then serve it at once.

NOTE FROM LAINE AND STEVE:

We chose this recipe for you because who would dream that mixing up these ingredients would make something that would double in size? Your relationship can grow immensely, deeply, exponentially, when you put ingredients into it with just the right heart. And if the soufflé falls, burns, or flops, you can always start again from scratch.

Dinner is Served

"The keynote to happiness within the four walls that make any home is plain, wholesome, well cooked food, attractively served."
Louis P. De Gouy, *The Soup Book* (1949)

CHAPTER TEN

Have Your Cake and Eat It Too

The Proof Is in the Pudding

"This isn't happily ever after. It's so much more than that."
Kiera Cass

*"And they lived happily (aside from a few normal
disagreements, misunderstandings, pouts, silent treatments,
and unexpected calamities) ever after."*
Jean Ferris

What are some of your favorite dishes? What makes your mouth water every time you walk in the door to the delectable aroma of something sizzling on the stove or baking in the oven?

Is it a perfect steak?

A beautiful cake?

What food do you crave when you have not tasted it for a while? What makes you literally close your eyes and sigh when you take the first bite?

When Steve and I started again from scratch and then worked hard to create a new recipe for our relationship, it was like walking into a welcoming house at the end of an exhausting day and smelling something absolutely wonderful in the air. The sense of anticipation over what was to come made my heart (instead of my stomach) rumble with the thought of the upcoming pleasure.

On the other hand, have you ever walked into the house right after someone burned a bag of popcorn in the microwave? The smell is horrible. Or have you ever eaten a wonderful crab, lobster, or shrimp dinner and forgotten to take the garbage out right away? By the next morning, the stench is so powerful it fills the entire house.

Which marriage would you rather have? The one that makes you anticipate every good thing, or the one that makes you wrinkle your nose in disgust because it stinks to high heaven?

Either Steve or I could have said no to starting again, and our miracle moment would never have existed. Our marriage would have come to a pitiful, pathetic end in divorce court. Instead of the fairy godmother turning the pumpkin into an ornate carriage, we would have been turning our carriage back into a blackened, over-ripe pumpkin like the ones kids like to smash in the middle of the street. Not a pretty sight.

What are some of the things that could have caused us easily to refuse to create something new that night? Pride, hurt feelings, a misplaced desire for "justice," stubbornness, fear, mistrust, exhaustion, anger, resentment, or bitterness. Any one of those could have kept us from forgiving. But none of those would have been worth holding onto in the long run. None of those things is listed among the fruits of the Spirit, for good reason. None of those negative emotions are tasty fruit.

If the walls you have built to keep your spouse out of your heart are so high that you don't know how to tear them down, know right now that you don't have to tear them down. All you have to do is simply surrender. You must give God everything. I had so much guilt, shame, resentment, anger, layers of hurts, brokenness, and lack of faith. I had to get to the end of me where God was my only hope. I can remember saying, "God, if you are for real then you better show up now." I had to give over every area of my life inside and out.

"All you have to do is *simply* surrender."

You do too. Tell God you will give up your right to those bad feelings. Tell Him you need Him to make you willing to start again from scratch. If you do, the walls will come down on their own. When we fall at the feet of God and offer our entire lives, the good, bad, and ugly, then God is free to now act on our faith and love for Him. The benefits are beyond compare.

The law, our culture, the media, the attorneys, and maybe even some of your friends and family make divorce sound good. Right. Easy. We live in a no-fault divorce era. It's not anyone's fault. We just have "irreconcilable differences." Right? Wrong. Let's take a good look at some of the "no-fault" consequences Steve and I would have gotten if we had divorced:

- Two mortgages or rental payments when we could barely afford one.

- Two sets of utilities.

- Loss of material goods, like furniture or cars.

- Loss of rejoicing in future payoffs of shared businesses, investments, or projects.

- Loss of some friends who would side with one of us or the other.

- Loss of social invitations from couples, as we would now be the awkward singles.

- Loss of any ties to the other spouse's family (in most cases, family sides with family).

- Loss of good standing in our church ministries.

- Ongoing ill will towards each other.

- Loneliness.

- Loss of any future memories together, like enjoying our children's graduations, weddings, and grandchildren.

- Loss of time with our kids as they went back and forth between us.

- Lack of decision-making power and control in parenting.

- Loss of shared memories of the past, like our children's births and our own wedding.

- Loss of the satisfaction that comes from doing the hard work of forgiving and restoring.

- Loss of the personal growth reviving our marriage caused us to undergo.

Here's what our three beautiful children who were just entering adolescence at the time of our marriage miracle could have gotten if we had divorced:

- Loss of their intact home.

- Loss of their school or church if we had to move.

- Loss of their friends if we had to move or if the friends did not understand what they were going through.

- Loss of time with both of their parents.

- Loss of shared memories with us if we didn't want to remember those times.

- Loss of the ability to go to college if divorce plunged us into more debt.

- Loss of activities, trips and material goods if we could not afford them because of the divorce.

- Anger, bitterness and resentment towards us.

- Confusion and pain.

- Mistrust that love or marriage can last.

- Loss of respect for us, their parents.

- Loss of space and comfort level in their new home if either Steve or I met and married someone else.

- Complications of a stepfamily.

- Pressure of pleasing two parents who do not agree on anything.

- Pressure of carrying parents' messages back and forth.

- Stress on special occasions like graduations and birthdays when both parents would have to be in the same room.

- Addictions, aggression, poor grades in school, or depression, which adolescents who experience divorce have higher rates of.

Sounds great, doesn't it? After reading all of that, who wouldn't want to start again from scratch?

It is counter to our culture today, but when we die to ourselves and give it all over to God we don't lose anything. We gain life. If you can make your marriage work, you don't lose anything. But most of the messages we hear in our culture say your marriage can't be revived or that you and the kids will be happier if you divorce. There is nothing further from the truth.

The effects of divorce are downplayed in our culture, but they are real. In a ten-year study by Judith S. Wallerstein of 113 children and adolescents from a largely white, middle-class population of divorced families in Northern California, the effects of divorce were found to be long-lasting. Ten years after the divorce, the young adults in the study still regarded their parents' divorce as a continuing major influence in their lives.

> "A significant number appear burdened by vivid memories of the marital rupture, by feelings of sadness, continuing resentment at parents, and a sense of deprivation."[1]

Instead of reaping any of those losses in our own lives or our kids', when Steve and I realigned our hearts and our priorities we soon found that other areas of struggle in our lives finally fell into place. When we let go of the old, we began to see the places where there was life in our marriage instead of death and it gave us hope. We can testify that when you truly begin to create something new, the benefits and blessings you will begin to see in your marriage will give you the most delicious life you ever dreamed.

We know, because the proof is in our pudding. We didn't just start our marriage again from scratch yesterday or last month or a year ago. We began creating a whole new dish with fresh ingredients twelve years ago. It started with confessing our need for God, then confessing our failures to each other. Next came forgiveness and a brand new warmth of unconditional love that started heating up our hearts' ovens. Then came the cooking process. Over the next eighteen months of counseling, date nights and practicing new communication habits and quality time, our marriage began to give off some great-smelling scents. What we were surprised to discover was that our circumstances began to change too.

"When we let go of the old, we began to see the places where there was *life* in our marriage instead of death and it gave us hope."

We not only kept our home and businesses intact, but also we began to prosper. We felt like the man described by Jesus in Matthew 25:14-21. In this parable Jesus says,

> "Again, it will be like a man going on a journey, who called his servants and entrusted his wealth to them. To one he gave five bags of gold, to another two bags, and to another one bag, each according to his ability. Then he went on his journey. The man who had received five bags of gold went at once and put his money to work and gained five bags more. So also, the one with two bags of gold gained two more. But the man who had received one bag went off, dug a hole in the ground and hid his master's money.
>
> After a long time the master of those servants

returned and settled accounts with them. The man who had received five bags of gold brought the other five. 'Master,' he said, 'you entrusted me with five bags of gold. See, I have gained five more.' "His master replied, 'Well done, good and faithful servant! You have been faithful with a few things; I will put you in charge of many things. Come and share your master's happiness!'"

"The man with two bags of gold also came. 'Master,' he said, 'you entrusted me with two bags of gold; see, I have gained two more.' "His master replied, 'Well done, good and faithful servant! You have been faithful with a few things; I will put you in charge of many things. Come and share your master's happiness!'

"Then the man who had received one bag of gold came. 'Master,' he said, 'I knew that you are a hard man, harvesting where you have not sown and gathering where you have not scattered seed. So I was afraid and went out and hid your gold in the ground. See, here is what belongs to you.'

"His master replied, 'You wicked, lazy servant! So you knew that I harvest where I have not sown and gather where I have not scattered seed? Well then, you should have put my money on deposit with the bankers, so that when I returned I would have received it back with interest.'" (NIV)

We feel like that story is pretty clear. If God trusts you with something, you need to make it grow. God is looking for harvest. He gives opportunities, and we are to help people see Him through them. God trusted us with keeping our promise of marriage for life to each other. For a long time, we did not show ourselves trustworthy of that responsibility. Our marriage did not grow; it withered almost to nothing. We didn't take good care of the gift God had given us in each other. When we showed Him we could honor our promises to each other and Him, we believe God decided He could begin to trust us with other things.

Everything we do in life is supposed to be for the glory of God. That basically means to make Him look good because He is so good to us, so that others will want to get to know Him and experience His abundant life too. When we become trustworthy in little things, God can give us bigger things to handle.

Within two years of our marriage miracle, He gave us something bigger to handle. Bigger than our wildest dreams. Suddenly, we experienced a miracle of a different kind.

A great, big miracle known as wisdom, wealth, and Black Gold to boot.

For a long time, I did not understand why God would allow me to work so hard, giving 110 percent and receiving what looked like nothing in return. I had invested and spent everything I had. College, graduate school, including 127 credit hours of geology, physics, calculus, and geophysics. I graduated into an industry experiencing active layoffs and firings. So with my degree hot off the presses and zero dollars in the bank, I formed a construction company. My first job gave me a profit of 400 dollars, the company's first "working capital." I dedicated myself to getting jobs and completing them right. In one year, the company completed 55 commercial and residential jobs. I now had 40,000 dollars in the bank. Enough to live on for one year, so now I could try to start and build an oil company.

Starting an oil company was more complex than I ever imagined. It meant learning a whole lot more than my college classes ever taught me. Taxes, bookkeeping, law, environmental law, mineral law, deeds and trusts, federal regulations, state regulations, special regulations, securities laws and licenses, computers (something we didn't have in college), insurance, W-2 forms and employee laws, engineering, contracts, leases, contouring and map making and drafting through black line, then air brush, then autocad, log interpretation, and more, all self-taught. For some reason, others already in the oil business did not care to share knowledge with new oil companies.

That was just the beginning. In my first year, I learned that the main company in Dallas who bought deals purchased about 120 each year, but I also learned that they looked at about 1,200 proposals. Nine out of 10 deals went into the garbage can. At least I was smart enough to ask. That meant all of my work must be in the top 10 percent. I studied every prior well drilled in any county of interest. I had to finance the seismic formation acquired by the major oil companies for our use. I had to understand the oil layers that formed over time and unravel ever-evolving computer algorithms that assist in properly understanding the returns of sound waves recorded by a seismic acquisition truck in 1969.

After all this, I felt a little unraveled myself. It took 18-hour days, weekends, holidays. Each project like starting a new business several times a year for almost two decades. Each deal came with new contracts, partners, cities to travel to. Houston, Dallas, New Orleans, San Antonio, Ft. Worth. I sometimes showed a deal to as many as 100 companies to secure funding.

All of that careful planning and timing, only to come up empty time and again. I knew that if larger oil companies were buying my deals, they must think the deals were good, but my disappointment grew every time another initial test well came up dry. Calling everyone involved with the news of a dry hole was hard. Phone calls prevailed because the Internet, email, and even fax machines were not yet invented.

I thought surely it would only take three projects to find success, five at the most. I recall a specific prayer I voiced in my second year of the oil business. I was driving to Houston, crossing the long bridge across the Atchafalaya River between Baton Rouge and Lafayette, when I said, "God, we don't have any good prospects, nor ideas, nor even any seismic to work with. If you will just give me three deals out of this trip, I will take it from there."

I prayed, but we didn't hit. Not for a long time. It took more than forty projects, with only a few that worked, but not in a way that was enough to matter. Now I know how naive it was for me to tell God to give me three and I would handle it from there. My "handling" came up empty. When I gave everything to God as part of our marriage restoration, the restoration brought one hundred great oil wells in as many months, something unheard of in the oil industry, nearly statistically impossible.

My naive prayer was really, really bad. God is really, really good. I now know that I am still creating ideas and deals, some fifty deals later, from that same trip, that same prayer. He answered with many, many more than three. I could have saved a lot of time if I had followed God's advice twenty years sooner.

If you are experiencing setbacks in your life and still have not made a true connection with God, I challenge you to get on the same page with Him now. I am a scientist through and through. Science and Christianity are often painted as being at odds. But I can prove God's existence through science and the scientific method. In chemistry class, for example, if an experiment works once, then you must repeat it. The scientific method means that a specific result is proven by "repetition of result." The same outcome over and over and over again.

In my life, the outcomes repeated themselves again and again and again. When I tried to handle everything myself, I came up empty year after year after year. When I gave everything to God and let Him be in charge, the blessings repeated so often some-

times I ask Him now to give favor to someone else because I can hardly handle so much. The repetition and occurrences in my life cannot be coincidence, as the calculations would be statistically impossible.

I wonder why we humans try so hard to do it all ourselves. I spent my first forty years. Are you kidding me? Now I realize I spent the same amount of time wandering in my personal desert of no returns after my simple prayer to God as the Israelites did wandering in the desert after leaving their slave years behind in Egypt. God rescued them from slavery in a huge way by parting the Red Sea. Then they started complaining to God and began trying to do it all themselves, going round and round right outside the Promised Land. Why did they do that? Why waste forty years? Why did I? Why don't we all learn sooner?

We hope that by creating the new "recipes" in this book for your marriage, you can learn a better way much sooner than we did. You can save yourself tons of grief and heartache. Do you have a voice in the back of your head telling you to hand it over? I know I did. I know God told me over and over to read the New Testament. "Just read it. It's free. Read it now before you waste your whole life trying to do it all by yourself," He said. Finally, I started obeying.

After I hit my lowest point and God lifted me from the depths of hell in our garage, I slowly began to see pinpoints of light. And on the forty-second prospect, it happened. We hit the hidden treasure underground. The new oil find hit big. Bigger than I could have dreamed. You see, most new oil finds have one to three wells. This one hit twenty-five, then fifty, then eighty. It just kept coming. Suddenly, every well I drilled worked. Success became an understatement. And by the time that year was up and the oil came, Laine and I had enough time invested in the marriage we had started again from scratch to stand side-by-side, enjoying the blessings.

If Laine and I had split up that fateful night in the garage, it might never have happened. If it had, I would have become a wealthy playboy. I could have afforded the Maserati and more. But I would not have had the wife of my youth by my side to enjoy the payoff. The woman who had worked with me all these years. The one who gave me our beautiful kids. The huge score would have been an empty one at best.

But eighteen months after our initial turning point, the feelings of failure had lifted. Our finances did a complete turnaround. We were no longer scraping the bottom of the barrel just to get by. Now we had enough money not only to live well, but also to give to others. We could begin helping family members, giving more to God's work, and discovering what we could invest in so we could further His kingdom.

God more than fulfilled his promise in Acts 3:19, which says this: "So you must change your hearts and lives! Come back to God, and he will forgive your sins. Then the Lord will send the time of rest." (NCV)

That's exactly what happened. After all those years of trying to make it work under our own force of will, our own efforts, our own ambition, all Laine and I had gotten was exhaustion. As soon as we changed our hearts and lives and came back to God, He forgave us and sent the time of rest.

That's another part of the paradox of Christian living. The Bible says it is only when you give up your life that you truly gain it. I believe it, because I am living it. When I gave up my right to my sinful alternative life as a single man, and I committed fully to one course only, I gave God room to work. God witnessed my choice, and then I did what God was telling me to do all along (and if you don't know what this is, read the New Testament).

I took a small step towards God, which freed Him to take His big step in my life. Bam! His steps are huge. I believe God likes to show off to the ones He loves. Blessings everywhere. So I took another small step. Just like stepping over a small ditch, jumping just a little to reach the other side, He requires you to stretch and

189

take a little risk each time. Bam! God had me covered before I hit the other side. I was safe with Him.

All He asks is that you listen, follow, and give Him the credit. He said to me two things: "Rest and tell everyone who really did all of this for you." As you get more confident in your faith, you can take bigger steps. But you can't outstep God. His steps are ten-fold yours. You can't outdo Him. He is really quite unbelievable!

Within five years of our revived marriage, we moved from our modest home to our dream house, a 10,000-square-foot estate home on twenty-five acres. I had woods to walk in, a garden to tend, a pool to swim in, and a lake to enjoy. We could entertain, have people visit, and enjoy being surrounded by beauty. The church used our grand parlor for meetings. My wife now had the freedom to follow her call to minister to other women.

"You can't outstep God. His steps are ten-fold yours. You can't *outdo* Him."

We didn't have to fight anymore about who was working harder or which bill to pay. We could now afford to send our kids to college.

Now don't get the wrong idea about all this. The miracle was not the money or the things it could buy us. The miracle was our relationship, with or without the money. The money would have meant nothing except one more thing to fight over and split in half if Laine and I had not made it. The money makes life easier in many ways, but it comes with its own challenges and responsibilities too. Some people might think when you make a lot of money all you do is sit by the pool living in the lap of luxury. But we have found that when much is given, much is expected. God has plenty for us to do. And we still have to do all of the things everyone else does. We take care of kids, accounts, taxes, family members, friends, lawns and weeds, along with all of the new projects and ministries that God gives us, too many to list.

In some ways, there is more work to do now, not less. God's blessings do not mean you can hoard them, sitting on a lounge chair drinking margaritas. I expect if you stop taking steps to increase your faith, God's steps will get smaller too. God gives us wealth to use for Him. We love our dream house, but it is for a season and it belongs to God for His purposes.

We found a miracle buried under a pile of junk stashed away and forgotten in the garage. Not the carjacks, old bikes, and tools. No, the real pile of junk was the doubt, fear, and distrust. When we dug it all out and gave it to God, underneath it all we discovered our truest treasure: trust, forgiveness, truth, honesty, and courage. We rediscovered love.

When we found these and gave them to each other, God grew them. After such a long season of not honoring the gift God had given us in our marriage, now we had proven ourselves worthy of the tremendous covenant. Now God was evidently willing to trust us with finances that could bless others.

Many people witnessed what God did for us. They were intrigued. Some were jealous. Some felt like it wasn't fair that we got the blessing and they didn't. But we wrote this book because a lot of people asked us how they could do it too. Not just achieve wealth, but also restore their relationships with God, their spouse, and their family. We knew we had a recipe too good to keep in the family. It needed to be shared.

People ask me, "Why did God answer your prayers? He doesn't answer mine. Why does He give you seconds, thirds, and fourths when I can't even get firsts?"

It's not because we are better than anyone else. We are no better than you. In fact, we were probably worse. We believe blessings continue to come because we continue to ask expectantly, give richly, and steward these gifts well. God expects us to take big leaps of faith, so He can come through in a big way. We are convinced He does not usually plop big, finished projects right in your lap so you can ride off into the sunset and enjoy a happy life doing nothing more than pleasing yourself.

No, God gives you blessings that need your hands and feet. The more we do, the more He does. The more we trust, the more He comes through. Remember, every morning I say, "Good morning, God. With you I am strong. I will walk without fear. And, God, by the way, is there anything I can do for you today?"

It's not about what He can do for us, but what we can do to be part of His plan. If you want God's voice to be heard in your life, if you want Him to show up in a big way, you have to be available. Can you ask God with a true heart, "What can I do for you today, God?" A true heart means you can't tell Him no when He answers you.

Are you afraid if you ask He might give you something you don't want to do? Or maybe something you don't think you can do? Are you scared of His plan? I was until I knew that fear was handed to men by the devil himself. Read the Bible and you'll see.

"If you want God's voice to be *heard* in your life, if you want Him to show up in a big way, you have to be available."

God's path is destined and can be trusted to be the best for you, but you often have to walk His path blindly. It is not for us to know God's ways, just to trust. That's the tough part. Keep the control and the fear and continue to operate miserably on your own? Or take bigger and bigger blind steps of faith, growing in confidence as God shows up and shows off in your life?

After more than fifteen years of working night and day, we were able to buy a penthouse in our favorite spot in Florida. We sit on the balcony and watch the beautiful waves of the Gulf of Mexico crash on the white sandy beaches. It's a place of refuge where Laine can take long walks along the shore to think and pray, and where we can watch dolphins swim and play. We enjoy "tasting and seeing" that the Lord is good. But we never forget for a second that it is all His, to be used to bring Him glory.

Today, I continue my oil work, but I apply the gift He has given me for loving the land and the layers of rock and the treasure underneath with the principles He has taught me about love, trust, forgiveness, and stewardship. I want to lift others up, trusting that God can bless all of us, rather than bring them down by unfair practices and cutthroat competition.

The world is a big place with much to do, much to create, much to build. I still love seeing what others fail to see in my four-dimensional, jigsaw-puzzle recreations of shorelines. Sometimes we see something no one else has seen and put thousands of acres of land under lease and drill. Occasionally, it's a dry hole and we start again, but more often than not now it's a gusher.

Finding a new oil field is like bringing something long dead to life again, just like God did for my life and my marriage. It's my gift, I believe, and I love being a geologist. God has gotten rid of generational "curses" and is creating a legacy of blessing. From my dad to me. And now from me to my kids.

My two sons are also geologists, and my oldest son recently joined the Craft Companies. Because we kept our family together, my boys love and respect me enough to work by my side. That may be the greatest gift I will ever be given. I could not ask for more. My oldest son told his mom the other day, "I knew I would enjoy working with my dad, but I didn't know how much." He has told me he is proud of me for staying married, proud of us for keeping our family together.

"You and Mom staying married kept me from a lot of temptations," my son said. "I know I got into some trouble, but if y'all had *gotten a divorce, I expect I would have gotten into drugs or totally self-destructed like so many of my friends. I am so glad that didn't happen, Dad." No fast car or fast woman could ever compare to those words from my firstborn.*

As for my sweet wife, God gave Laine a dream to reach women who feel as desperate as she once did. Whether women are struggling in their marriages, finances, drugs, or other circumstances, Laine lets them know they can be restored. My wife has a burning desire to tell women about our marriage revival and share with them the good news that Jesus can change their lives too. With God-given wealth, Laine has been able to develop that vision and make it come true in a big way. We receive countless emails that bring floods of tears as we read how the message of hope spread through local meetings, Laine's WHOAwomen Magazine, *or websites prevented suicides, stopped an abortion, saved a family member, or brought a beloved father to God just before he died.*

I have known God had a call on my life since I was a little girl. I have always loved to talk and share. I have no fear of public speaking, and practiced commercials and television shows into a pretend microphone when I was just a preschooler. I have always felt different, always itched to fulfill a big dream.

After our marriage miracle, I began asking God to show me what my purpose was for Him. What could I give back to Him for all He had done for us? That's when He told me to pay it forward. He gave me a dream to reach women who are lost and hurting. Not church women or Christian women, necessarily. But women trudging through their jobs, frustrated with their husbands, or trying to make it as single parents. Women who need the good news that they can be healed from their hurts, habits, and hangups.

So I went out and rented a hotel conference room, made up

some flyers and started advertising the "Brown Bag Bible Buddies" meetings. The idea was pretty simple. I would host one-hour lunch meetings so working women could come. I would hold them in a hotel instead of a church so women from all walks of life would not feel intimidated. We would eat lunch and hear a testimony of how God was working in women's lives today. Women could share with each other. Then we would leave encouraged as we went about the rest of our day.

The Brown Bag Bible Buddies became so popular that women in other cities and states began contacting me, wanting to start meetings in their area. As the local gatherings grew, my dream expanded. Lives were being changed, and I wanted to reach even more women with a message of hope.

With Steve's backing and at great expense, I launched the nationally circulated *WHOAwomen Magazine* in 2010. The glossy, quarterly publication contains articles from top counselors, authors, speakers and celebrities of faith who impart messages of hope and healing. It also contains fashion and home decor, topics women love. It addresses inner and outer beauty in a way that invites women into its welcoming warmth.

> "Lives were being *changed,* and
> I wanted to reach even more women
> with a message of hope."

I changed the name of the Brown Bag Bible Buddies gatherings to WHOAwomen Local, and soon the WHOA ministries reached around the world. In the past seven years, Steve and I have invested every dollar God has asked us to give into WHOAwomen Ministries. The magazine has not made a profit in money, but we receive letters and emails from all over the world telling us what a positive difference it has made in readers' lives. That makes every penny invested worth it.

I want to live by 1 Peter 3:15, which says:

> "But respect Christ as the holy Lord in your hearts.
> Always be ready to answer everyone who asks you
> to explain about the hope you have." (NCV)

He has given me so much, how can I not share it? Today, through the magazine, I get to spend time with celebrities for our cover stories, stand on red carpets at awards shows, and go behind the scenes on major television and film productions. I am having the time of my life, building new relationships and watching God heal hearts. And I have vowed always to be ready to explain the hope I have in Him.

In a time when more than half of all marriages are ending in divorce, and many of those who stay together do so unhappily, Steve and I know we have something rare. And beautiful. Our good news is that it doesn't have to be rare. We want our story to become commonplace. We want our shared testimony to show other couples they can do it too.

That's why we sat down together to write this book. To take the harvest to a whole new level. This story is a true labor of love. We hired a writer to help us get our thoughts down, found a designer to make the pages look pretty, created a website for you to go to for additional resources, www.startagainfromscratch.com, and had a fun day shooting the cover shot just for you. We prayed over each couple who would read this book and worked hard to get the word out so those who needed it could find it.

Along the way, God affirmed and reaffirmed what we were writing. Maybe that sounds sort of mystical to you, but it isn't weird at all. When you do what God wants you to do, it's like He pulls back the curtain and suddenly you get to see clearly the different ways He is working in your life. He lets you in on what

He is making happen behind the scenes.

Here's one example. A couple of years ago, I met some folks from the *700 Club*, a big Christian television show. They heard me talk about our marriage miracle, and they wanted to interview us and tell our story. They let me know it might be a long time before they would come tape us, maybe even a year. As months went by, I wasn't sure if they were serious or not. But I knew our story had hope in it for others. So I asked Steve if we could step out on faith, and we began writing this book.

Wouldn't you know it? Just as we got started on the book the *700 Club* called. They wanted to come to our Mississippi home to film, and the timing could not have been more perfect. The interview would air right around the time the book would be ready. God's hand was clearly at work. And I got to go along for the ride, basking in His glory and goodness.

The interview went great, and Steve and I enjoyed sitting together to share our no-fail recipe for reviving your marriage. It was even better because my best friend, the writer working with us on the book, the producer, reporter, and photographer all got to sit down and enjoy a meal at our table after the taping was done. We laughed and talked over gumbo, salad, and a chocolate brownie batter pie. The meal was delicious, and as I looked around the table I could so clearly "taste and see" that the Lord is good. Very good.

Personal friends who read early versions of the book said it helped them overcome some of the struggles they had been facing in their own marriages. We knew from the first stages the power these principles have to heal. When you allow God to transform your life, you get to be the catalyst for miracles in other people's lives. And that is so cool!

Today, Steve and I can't wait to see where He will take us next. God always keeps us on our toes. It's one grand adventure after the next. I am considering offers for a television show, WHOAwomen live conference events, and guest speaking opportunities with other ministries. I am launching my own brand, Livin' Lively with Laine. I want to share my story on the biggest platform I can find, not to see my name in lights, but in order for others to find the hope and healing I have found. It's life-changing. It's inspiring. And it makes all the difference in the world.

When Laine and I got our marriage back, we got everything back. We didn't have to experience any of those losses listed earlier. We got to keep everything intact and grow. When we hit oil, greed didn't have to rear its ugly head. I didn't have to scheme and plot and find ways to keep my ex-wife from getting her hands on it. Instead, I got to rejoice and celebrate with my bride and our family.

When you move past all the ugliness and hurt and begin creating a new recipe for your marriage, you get to have your cake and eat it too. And it's sweet, oh so sweet.

While Laine has found many opportunities to reach out publicly to women, I share my faith and our story more quietly behind the scenes for the most part. I love talking to men I meet in my business, sharing with them the lessons I have learned. I ask God to show me opportunities to share with others in my everyday life. It doesn't require a platform or spotlight, just a willingness to look for those who are hurting, listen to their stories, and lend your wisdom when they let you.

Writing this book with Laine was something totally new for me, and I found that I truly enjoyed sharing my voice. It's not too often that we men get taken seriously anymore, it seems like. Men are portrayed on television as violent and abusive or as ignorant fools. But a man who follows after God's own heart, protecting his marriage and family, is neither. He is a son of the most high God. A son of the King of Kings. A prince who will inherit God's kingdom.

On earth, I think that means we get to share in the fruits of our labor. When we work hard for God's glory, we get to bask in the light of that glory. Like Laine said, we get to "taste and see" that God is good. So my words here are written with all you husbands in mind. If you want courage for this, the biggest fight of your life, if you want to taste and see for yourself, then prepare for battle. Read God's Word. Pick up books like John Eldredge's Wild at Heart. *Do the hard work of counseling and date nights. Be a real man and start to fight for your marriage. Stop fighting to destroy it and go on an all-out rampage to keep it and make it whole.*

"When we work hard for God's *glory*, we get to bask in the light of that glory."

It will be the toughest but most enjoyable adventure of your lifetime. Don't fear change because it is unfamiliar. Remember, the familiar hasn't been that great. Get rid of your fears. Face them and defeat them one at a time. It is glorious and freeing to discover who you are created to be, to find your purpose and passion in God and with your wife by your side to cheer you on.

You will soon be filled with God-given anticipation and excitement to see what's around the next corner. That's a whole lot better than dreading the worst is about to hit. You were created in God's image to be like Him, so get to it. Stand up, stand strong, take back what satan tried to take from you.

Find your God-given path and get on it. Be bold and begin leading your family. Help your wife. Teach your kids. Don't leave anyone behind on this new journey toward abundant life. Divorce is not the only option. In fact, it should not be an option at this point at all. Fight for your marriage. Fight for your wife. Fight for your kids. After all, you are really fighting for yourself.

And if you apply this no-fail recipe and revive your marriage, you will have your own story to share. It will be a powerful one, too good, too rich to keep it all to yourself.

Then you can invite a struggling couple over, cook up something from the recipes within these pages, and talk about what God has done for you. It costs nothing to pay forward the hope you have found. You may discover you are the only help or hope that couple has been offered. You may be the difference between marriage miracle and devastating divorce. That's when you truly get to see that the proof is in the pudding.

Are you excited to see what God has in store for you next? Hopeful about your marriage restoration and ready to go to the next level and become *sous chefs*, preparing meals for others to enjoy? We hope so. When you pay it forward, you get to experience the power of your miracle again and again.

New York author Jesse Browner sums up the power of sharing a meal like this: "Eating and hospitality in general, is a communion," Browner said, "and any meal worth attending by yourself is improved by the multiples of those with whom it is shared."

> "When you pay it forward,
> you get to experience the power of
> your miracle again and again."

Ain't that the truth? Like Steve and I shared earlier, when we sit around the table with the ones we love, eating a good meal and sharing laughter and chitchat, there is nothing better in this world. Connected hearts, connected lives, tasting and seeing. *Mmm, mmm good!*

Now it's your turn, and we are absolutely ecstatic for you. Remember the recipe way back in "Chapter One: Burnt to a Crisp"? You know, the one for that Burnt Butter Frosting? At the beginning of this book, there was no cake to put it on.

Now, we think you are ready to have your cake and eat it too. So turn the page, read the recipe for life, add your own no-fail tweaks on the recipe card page, and then enjoy baking my mother's Southern pound cake. Whip up a batch of that frosting, and taste and see how sweet life can be. As a bonus, we're also including my famous Banana Pudding. Because the proof is in the pudding now. Prepare this creamy delight and make your marriage just as sweet. We're cheering you on every step of the way.

Bon appetit!

The Proof Is in the Pudding: Our No-Fail Recipe

INGREDIENTS:

1 newly revived married couple

Other couples in need of this no-fail recipe

Prayers

1 large table

Scrumptious treats or meals to share

Open eyes, listening ears, words of wisdom, to taste

DIRECTIONS:

Take the newly revived couple and refine their marriage miracle story. Pray for opportunities to share with others in need. The newly revived couple should keep their eyes open and their ears listening daily.

Pray for opportunities to tell of the life-changing work God has done in your lives. Tell your story wherever God leads, whether it's privately to a colleague or on a stage in front of hundreds.

Set your table and invite others to dine with you. Let them taste and see that the Lord is good and the proof is in your pudding!

The Proof Is in the Pudding:
Our No-Fail Recipe Card

From the Kitchen of: _____

INGREDIENTS:

_____

_____

_____ —

_____

_____

_____

_____

DIRECTIONS:

_____

_____

_____

_____

_____

_____

_____

_____

My Momma's Pound Cake

Now is the time to have your cake and eat it, too!
The Burnt Sugar Frosting from Chapter One adds the
final touch to this cake.

INGREDIENTS:

2 sticks butter

2 cups sugar

1 3/4 cups all-purpose flour

Dash of salt

1 teaspoon vanilla

6 eggs at room temperature

1 recipe for Burnt Butter Frosting (see Chapter One, page 28)

DIRECTIONS:

Combine sugar and butter in large bowl. Beat until light and creamy. Then add eggs one at a time with a little flour, beating between each addition until all the eggs and flour have been added. Add salt and vanilla and beat 10 minutes—you can overbeat it!

Pour batter into greased tube cake pan, and bake at 350 degrees for 50 to 60 minutes.

Let the cake cool in the pan on wire rack for 5 minutes. Then, flip it over to remove pan, and let it cool on the wire rack.

Prepare Burnt Butter Frosting, and drizzle over cooled cake.

The Best Banana Pudding

INGREDIENTS:

1 (5-ounce) package vanilla instant pudding mix

2 cups cold milk

1 (14-ounce) can sweetened condensed milk

1 tablespoon vanilla extract

1 (12-ounce) container frozen whipped topping, thawed

1 (16-ounce) package vanilla wafers

14 bananas, sliced

DIRECTIONS

In a large mixing bowl, beat pudding mix and milk 2 minutes. Blend in condensed milk until smooth. Stir in vanilla and fold in whipped topping. Layer wafers, bananas and pudding in a glass serving bowl. Chill until serving.

NOTE FROM LAINE AND STEVE:

We are so glad you joined us in the kitchen to cook up our no-fail recipe to revive your marriage. We hope you are on a new journey together to create some delicious days and yummy years to come. Now we want you to enjoy your cake and dive into this banana pudding. The rewards of a great marriage are sweet!

Endnotes

Chapter Three

1. Cohen, Elizabeth. "Blaming Others Can Ruin Your Health." *CNN.com.* N.p., 18 Aug. 2011. Web. 12 Jan. 2015. <http://www.cnn.com/2011/HEALTH/08/17/bitter.resentful.ep/>.

2. "Adult Health." Forgiveness: Letting Go of Grudges and Bitterness. Mayo Clinic, n.d. Web. 6 Dec. 2014. <http://www.mayoclinic.org/healthy-living/adult-health/in-depth/forgiveness/art-20047692>.

Chapter Five

1. Smith, Emily E. "Masters of Love." *Theatlantic.com.* The Atlantic, 12 June 2014. Web. 23 Dec. 2014. <http://www.theatlantic.com/health/archive/2014/06/happily-ever-after/372573/>.

Chapter Nine

1. "Falling in Love with Your Husband Again." Personal interview of Jamie Garcia by Natalie N. Gillespie. 16 May 2006.

Chapter Ten

1. Wallerstein, Judith S. "Children of Divorce: Preliminary Report of a Ten-Year Follow-up of Older Children and Adolescents." Journal of the American Academy of Child Psychiatry 24.5 (1985): 545-53. Web. 2 Feb. 2015.

Dear Wonderful Readers,

We can't tell you how glad we are that you wanted to revive your marriage enough to pick up our book. We pray you found it helpful, encouraging, and transforming. We want you to know our marriage is still going strong. Our children are among our best friends, and we love to work, play, and pray together.

Life always brings challenges, but now Steve and I face those difficult times together, shoulder-to-shoulder against the world and on our knees before God. We hope you will do the same with your spouse from today forward.

Know we are praying for every couple who reads this book. We are standing on God's promises for your marriage. Will you pray for us too? Since the writing of this book, oil prices have been cut in half which greatly affects our income, my Dad has dementia, I had skin cancer removed, and more. Now these are real challenges!

Still, we stand firm in our faith, faithful in our marriage, waiting to see what God has for us next. We don't know what it will be, but we know we can trust Him. We know He has good plans for us, so we can have hope and a future (Jeremiah 29:11).

Whatever challenge comes your way, remember God has a hope and a future for you and your marriage too. We know He does, and we pray He will continue to show up and show off in your lives in a big way.

If *Start Again from Scratch* helped you, we humbly ask you to help us spread the word. Post a review on Amazon.com. Pass a copy of this book to another couple in need. And please get in touch. We want to hear from you and get to know your story. You can connect with us in many ways to see what we are up to next. We guarantee it will be an adventure!

Check out our website at StartAgainfromScratch.com and sign up for our monthly newsletter. Follow us on Twitter @LainewithSteve, Like us on our Start Again from Scratch Facebook page, and take a look at our YouTube channel Start Again from Scratch.

Now, put this book down and go cook up some good lovin'!

Livin' Lively,
Laine Lawson Craft

The gift that gives –
all year long